W9-AHU-682

**BALLET BASICS**

# BALLET BASICS

## THIRD EDITION

**Sandra Noll Hammond**
University of Hawaii

Mayfield Publishing Company
Mountain View, California
London • Toronto

Copyright © 1993, 1984, 1974 by Mayfield Publishing Company
Third edition

All rights reserved. No portion of this book may be reproduced in
any form or by any means without written permission of the publisher.

Library of Congress Cataloging-in-Publication Data
Hammond, Sandra Noll.
    Ballet basics / Sandra Noll Hammond. — 3rd ed.
       p.     cm.
    Includes bibliographical references and index.
    ISBN 1–55934–134–3
    1.  Ballet dancing.   I.  Title.
  GV1788.H35   1993
  792.8 — dc20                             92–19098
                                             CIP

Manufactured in the United States of America

10   9   8   7   6   5   4

Mayfield Publishing Company
1240 Villa Street
Mountain View, California 94041

Sponsoring editor: Erin Mulligan; production editor, Sondra Glider;
manuscript editor, Betty Duncan; art director, Jeanne M. Schreiber;
illustrators, Robin Mouat, Diana Thewlis; manufacturing manager, Martha
Branch.

The text was set in 10/12 Zapf International by Thompson Type and printed
on 50# Finch Opaque by Banta Company.

# CONTENTS

# PREFACE

The popular image of the beginning ballet student is that of a knobby-kneed eight- or ten-year-old girl, eyes sparkling with dreams of becoming a ballerina. This book, however, is written for the beginning ballet student who is at least eight years older than that dreamy-eyed child. For a variety of reasons this person, male or female, has enrolled in an adult beginning ballet class — in a department of physical education or fine arts at a college or university, in a community or arts center, in a private studio or professional dancing school. No matter where the ballet class meets, certain fundamental activities and protocol will be observed. This book can serve to introduce and explain the basic outline of the ballet class — the work at the *barre* and in the center, the dress and comportment of the student, the function of the classroom itself, and the role of the teacher.

The study of ballet as a means to a career as a professional ballet dancer is not very realistic for the adult beginner. There are a few, very rare, exceptions of talented latecomers who began the study of ballet in their late teens and eventually joined one company or another as professional dancers. But even those rare cases are almost always men who came to ballet after several years of training in other forms of dance (tap, jazz, or folk) or in a related activity such as gymnastics.

It is assumed, therefore, that the reader probably does not dream of becoming a professional ballet dancer. Is there a valid reason for an adult to study ballet? I believe the answer is yes and, moreover, a plural yes.

Ballet technique involves and challenges the entire body. Its intricacies and harmonies stimulate the mind as well as the muscles. For total body exercise it has few equals. The determined student even may discover performing, teaching, and choreographing opportunities in the ever-multiplying amateur groups, civic or regional. Ballet training is widely recognized as a valuable foundation for other dance forms in which there indeed may be professional performing careers for those beginning relatively late in life. Certainly new and expanded opportunities exist in ballet-related fields, for which an understanding of ballet technique is a benefit and often a requirement.

The execution of ballet technique can do more than exercise muscles and strengthen ligaments or provide an outlet for the performing urge. When done carefully and correctly, it can improve body posture and carriage and, eventually, the actual shape of the body. It can stimulate the appreciation of dance as a medium of expression, thus developing a more informed audience. Admittedly, progress in these directions may be slow in an adult after years of habitual careless posture, accumulated tensions, and desultory attendance at dance concerts. For the person who would attempt to correct such habits, the ballet classroom is one place to begin, the modern dance classroom being, of course, another.

A student who has chosen the ballet classroom will soon be immersed in an art rich in over five centuries of history, an art form worthy of serious study by an adult. The evolution of ballet is detailed in many fascinating books, but reading about ballet cannot begin to impart the excitement and understanding that study from a good classroom teacher can—a teacher whose expertise is part of that historical legacy. Books such as this one are offered as an aid to, not a substitute for, that study.

This third edition contains additional illustrations and expanded, updated material in each chapter. But the intention of the book remains the same: to provide an auxiliary source for the beginning-level ballet class by supplying information about basic ballet technique. In addition, the text offers suggestions on the care of the dancer's instrument—the body—a glimpse of the professional world of ballet, and a historical perspective.

I wish to thank my ballet instructors who, through the years, have indirectly helped me write this book, especially Margaret Craske and Antony Tudor, The Juilliard School and the Metropolitan Opera School of Ballet; Alan Howard, Pacific Ballet, San Francisco; Thalia Mara and Arthur Mahoney, School of Ballet Repertory, New York City; Dolores Mitrovich, Tucson, Arizona; and my very first teachers, Toby Jorgensen and Sue Keller, Fayetteville, Arkansas.

I also want to thank the following reviewers for their thoughtful reading of a preliminary version of this edition: Stan Bobo, Stephen F. Austin State University; Judith Chazin-Bennahum, University of New Mexico; Laura Gurdus Dolid, Goucher College; Joetta Jercinovic, University of New Mexico; Jaye Knutson, Towson State University; Billie Mahoney, Northern Illinois University; Keitha Donnelly Manning, Louisiana School for Math, Science & the Arts; Myron Howard Nadel, Buffalo State College; Betty Swenson, Jacksonville University; and Maris Wolff, Johnson State College.

# CHAPTER 1

# THE BALLET CLASS

The necessary elements of any ballet-technique class—the teacher, the studio, the student, the music, the vocabulary—and the first procedures of the lesson are the subjects of this chapter.

Technique classes six days a week are expected of students preparing for a professional career in ballet, but two or three classes per week may be more realistic for the adult beginner who has a different dance goal in mind. However, the benefits of the daily ballet class regimen are hard to deny, especially in view of the fact that muscles do not retain their stretch or strength. It is sobering to realize that within twenty-four hours after activity ceases, muscle atrophy begins.

Thus, "taking class" is a regular part of the life of every dancer, no matter how advanced he or she is. It is the special time and place for continual artistic enrichment and personal discovery, as well as just day-to-day maintenance of the dance instrument itself—the body.

## THE TEACHER

Most important to a ballet class is a well-qualified teacher. Indeed, all ballet artists credit their success to one or more great teachers with whom they have studied. These teachers most probably had been dancers themselves at one time, an important consideration for students bent on a professional dance career. An often-heard maxim, "Great dancers aren't always great teachers," is true enough, but a gifted teacher (usually with experience as a performer and some

1

knowledge of classical ballet repertory) seems to be in the background of every great dancer.

The teacher of a beginning class for adults need not be a retired *prima ballerina* or *premier danseur* with firsthand acquaintance of famous ballet roles, but she or he should have a sound knowledge of ballet technique and an understanding of human anatomy. The instrument being trained is the human body; the teacher's job is, therefore, a complex and responsible one.

Knowing and showing the steps is not enough, especially for beginning classes. An exercise needs to be "broken down" into basic movements that must be mastered before the complete step is attempted. These slow, elementary exercises may seem totally unrelated to the brilliant footwork of dancers seen on stage and screen. Those serene artists show no signs of effort, sweat, or fatigue, but a visit backstage at a performance or to a professional class will quickly dispel the vision of effortless motion. To dance is to work, and to work very hard. It is the teacher's job to guide that work soundly, and the good teacher can make it exciting and enjoyable.

Teaching methods and manners vary. One teacher may be "dressed out" in practice clothes like the rest of the class; another may wear street clothes and shoes. One instructor may demonstrate every exercise; another will remain seated throughout the lesson. A teacher's voice may be loud, accompanied by hand clapping or finger snapping, or it may be soft, as though only two persons were in the studio. Many teachers employ a variety of styles and resort to a number of ways of reaching the students — serious, joking, angry, anecdotal.

Corrections and suggestions are basic ingredients to instruction, and a good teacher knows when and how to give them to the beginner as well as to the advanced dancer. Basically there are two kinds of correction — that given to the entire class and that given to an individual. Take heed of both! A soloist with a famous company has said that she always listened to a class correction as though it were said to her personally. When an individual correction is given, it should not be received as an embarrassing insult, and one hopes it was not offered in such a manner. Most teachers have a genuine interest in the progress of their pupils and a true dedication to ballet. A correction is considered an aid to progress, and the teacher is likely to lose interest in the student who ignores or systematically forgets corrections. If corrections apply to a serious structural problem and are still ignored, the student may be asked to withdraw from the class. Ballet technique is a powerful tool for building strong bodies, but when done incorrectly it is equally powerful in damaging them. The teacher of a beginning class for adults should not expect the technical perfection of a younger student enrolled in a professional ballet school. Neither should the adult who enrolls in a ballet class expect to float randomly around the room as music plays somewhere in the background.

Ballet's aristocratic heritage from royal courts has continued a certain formalism in manners as well as style. Thus, in class a certain politeness prevails, and the ballet teacher may expect to be addressed as Miss, Madame, or Mr. Such-and-Such even though some students in the class may be older than the teacher or on a first-name basis outside of class. Although this procedure may sound austere, it does not detract from the teacher's availability for answering serious questions and listening to individual problems. Adult classes offer both teacher and students the opportunity to discuss artistic and historical matters as well as technical concerns of ballet. The classroom should be a place to ask as well as to listen.

## THE STUDIO

The ballet classroom is an unpretentious place, for the needs of the class are simple, though specific. Typically the room is fairly large, often approximating the rectangular shape and size of a stage. A wooden floor is essential. Dancers prefer it to be "raised" (the boards resting on joists, or supports) so as to allow a certain give under the weight of the body. This slight cushioning effect helps reduce fatigue and prevent injuries that can occur from dancing on a concrete floor. The raised floor usually is made of hardwood with its surface smooth but not slick. A once-familiar sight before ballet class was the teacher sprinkling the floor with a watering can to prevent a slippery surface. Today, the wood floors of many studios and stages have vinyl coverings, such as Marly or Rosco-floors, that provide a smooth, nonslippery dance surface.

Every ballet studio contains *barres*, which are long railings made of wood or metal pipes, either attached to the walls or supported from the floor. A studio may also contain portable *barres*. Whether permanent or portable, they have to be steady, offering the student a secure place to begin the lesson. The average height of the *barre* from the floor is three feet, six inches, but obviously some adjustment can be made for the very short or very tall person. (See Chapter 2, "Use of the *Barre*," for further discussion of the relationship of the *barre* and the student.)

Usually at least one wall of the studio contains a mirror. Often one entire wall is covered by mirrors and designated the "front" of the room because the dancers usually face that wall when they leave the *barre* to do center work. The mirror allows the dancer to check instantly the correctness of a position or movement, but it can turn into another crutch, especially for the beginner. Students can become so accustomed to dancing before their own images that facing a nonmirrored wall leaves them at a loss. (This loss is nothing, however, compared with that felt by the dancer, trained and rehearsed in a mirrored studio, who first sets foot on a stage and looks out, not to mirrors but the blackness of the auditorium.) Focusing on the mirror can often distort a position and actually make some movements more difficult (especially turns). A teacher is wise to change, at least occasionally, the "front" of the room to a nonmirrored wall.

A studio needs to be well ventilated but not drafty and sufficiently warm to allow the muscles of the body to work easily. Few ballet facilities are luxurious, many are barely adequate, and some are depressingly dingy. But the art of ballet seems to transcend these surroundings as it passes from the careful teacher to the hard-working students, for ballet is not contained within the walls of the studio but within the body, mind, and spirit of the dancers.

## THE STUDENT

Enrollment in a beginning ballet class should — but often does not — depend on permission of the instructor after a personal interview. It is important for the teacher to know whether the student has any physical handicaps, particularly problems of the heart, spine, knees, or feet. This knowledge is especially significant for the admission of a child into the rigorous training program for professional ballet, but it is also important information to know about any student who takes ballet technique classes. Certain physical problems may not preclude ballet study, but they may temper the way training is approached.

### Clothing

Students admitted into a beginning ballet class will need certain equipment: tights, leotard, soft ballet shoes. Because of the great variety of dancewear now available, it is wise to check with the instructor for the preferred style and color of such items before purchasing them. In a college or university dance course, instructions about equipment often are given at the first class meeting.

Classroom dress for a woman means tights (usually pink), covering the body from feet to waist, and leotard (often black) worn over the tights from the hips to the shoulders. These practice clothes are made of a stretchable material that can be worn skintight while allowing full freedom of movement with the outline of the body seen clearly. This exposure is often an unnerving experience for the beginner, but it is vital for the teacher, who is concerned with correct placement and movement of the body. Actually, tights and leotard are much less revealing than a bathing suit. They soon begin to feel like a second skin and as appropriate for the study of ballet as a bathing suit is for swimming. It is unnecessary to wear underpants beneath the tights, but, if worn, they should be of bikini style and must never show below the leotard. The long line of the leg must not be shortened by the outline of an undergarment or by a leotard pulled down to an unflattering straight angle on the thigh. To prevent possible tearing of breast tissue, a well-fitting bra with nonstretching straps should be worn if bra size is 32B or more.

The male dancer wears heavier tights, often black, and a T-shirt tucked into the tights. Under the tights, he wears a dance belt of the same color as the tights, made of elastic and strong cloth, with the wide cloth part worn in front.

The dance belt gives more support and protection to the genitals than an ordinary athletic supporter. If a leotard is worn instead of a T-shirt, it is put on after the dance belt but before the tights. To prevent a baggy look, the tights must be pulled up so that they fit firmly at the crotch. They can be secured in this position by elastic suspenders attached to the top of the tights and carried over the shoulders; or a belt can be worn around the waist with the top of the tights rolled over it.

**Ballet Shoes**   Ballet dancing usually is associated with "toe dancing," but beginning students never wear toe shoes — dancers refer to them as point shoes. (See Chapter 5, "Care of the Feet," for guidelines for minimum requisites for dancing on *pointe*.) Beginners, both male and female, wear soft ballet slippers, made of leather or canvas, that have been constructed to give protection while allowing flexibility to the feet. Other soft shoes, such as gymnastic or jazz shoes, do not allow the feet to work properly in ballet exercises, nor do they give the correct "line" to the feet.

The ballet shoe gives the ballet dancer the best possible base from which to work; but it may feel strange indeed when first tried on! The shoe should fit the foot as snugly as a glove fits the hand, but there should still be room for the toes to lie flat, although there must never be extra space at the end of the toes as in a normal street shoe. (Long toenails can result in a misfitted shoe and/or painful bruising later on. See Chapter 5, "Minor Foot Ailments," for proper nail care.) An American-made ballet shoe is purchased usually at least one size, sometimes two sizes, smaller than a street shoe. Individual differences, such as a particularly long big toe, call for different considerations when buying or ordering ballet shoes. It is best to have the teacher check the fit before the student wears the shoes.

The teacher can also show where to sew on the elastic that will keep the heel of the shoe in place. Elastic strips usually come with ballet shoes, but they are seldom sewn on by the manufacturer. Many studios prefer women students to use satin ribbons instead (available at the same shoe store), which are tied around the ankle exactly as ribbons for point shoes. To determine the proper position for the ribbon or elastic on the shoe, fold the heel inward until it lies flat on the sole of the shoe. The elastic or ribbon should be sewn directly in front of this fold.

Like any other shoes, ballet shoes need to be broken in before they are worn for any length of time, such as a period of an entire class. After the teacher has checked the correctness of the fit, the shoes should be softened by bending them back and forth in the hands. Then they can be worn for short periods around the house, but never outside; the soles must be kept free from dirt that might track onto the studio floor.

There is no right or left to ballet shoes when they are new. Because the shoes are soft, however, and tend to mold to the feet, most dancers prefer not to switch them once the molding process has begun. The softness of the shoes also causes them to stretch with continual wear, and the resulting looseness can be adjusted by tightening the strings at the front of the shoe. These strings must never hang out but should always be tucked into the shoe. Professional ballet company members can be subject to fines if caught with dangling shoestrings or ribbons on stage.

## Care of Equipment

Getting outfitted for a ballet class involves initial expenses that often are hard on a student budget, but equipment bought for a first class should last for many years if it is properly used and cared for. The shoes, which will be the first item to wear out, should be removed immediately after class and allowed to air before being stored in a dance bag or locker. Because it is unwise and uncomfortable to keep wearing damp practice clothes after class, the student should shower immediately and change into dry clothes. After every class, the dance clothes should be washed in mild soap and warm water, with fabric softener added to prolong the stretchiness of the leotards and tights. The garments should be allowed to hang dry as they will shrink in the hot temperatures of most dryers.

**Accessories**   Students who continue in dance may want to add to their basic dance wardrobe. Dancers are fond of wearing many layers of dance clothing to concentrate heat where it is most needed, removing one or more of these layers as muscles get warm. The most frequent additions to the basic wardrobe are leg and ankle warmers, made of a wool or orlon knit and worn over the ordinary dance tights. A close-fitting sweater sometimes is worn, especially in cold weather. The current popularity of dance wear with the general public creates a vast selection of new styles and fabrics from which to choose. For class use, however, any dance garment should neither hinder the dancer's movement nor obstruct the clear outline of the body. Teachers frequently refuse to permit students, especially beginners, to wear sweat pants or shirts as a second layer. These bulky garments may feel cozy, but they also may hide serious technical faults or structural problems that can cause weakness or injury.

## Hair and Jewelry

Hair should be fastened securely to keep it off the face and neck. The distraction of hair falling into the eyes or whipping about the face in turns or jumps is acute for the student as well as the teacher. Practical aids such as headbands, hair clips or pins, or rubber bands should be used if the hair is long. This applies to men as well as women. When glasses are worn, it is advisable to secure them with a stretch-band, available at sporting goods stores. Try to keep jewelry to a minimum, not only for the important sake of a neat, uncluttered appearance but also for the sake of safety. Watches, large rings, dangling earrings, and bracelets can be hazardous and distracting to the wearer as well as to other dancers.

## Attendance

Proper equipment and grooming are necessary, but equally important is regular attendance in classes. Attendance should become a habit, for only by regular work will improvement be possible. If one day a student is "not feeling up to par," but is not really ill, perhaps arrangements can be made to observe class. A great deal is learned from watching others and from writing down the exercises they perform.

Taking a technique class in the evening, after a day of hard work, may require great discipline, but, more often than not, the body will respond surprisingly well and be revived by the workout. Exercises and stretches frequently make a person feel better, as is often the case for women with menstrual cramps. Dancers must—and students would do well to—continue their regular activities during menstruation. If a woman has to miss one class a month, she should, if possible, try to make it up in another section at the same technical level. If many absences occur, the body (and mind) will not be able to catch up with the rest of the class.

## Behavior in Class

More is expected, however, than merely bringing a body to class regularly, for ballet includes the intellectual and emotional being as well as the physical. Studying ballet requires full attention during class; it requires eyes and ears that are open for all available dance clues, a mouth that is closed to chatter (and empty of chewing gum), and a mind and body that are quietly ready for the work ahead.

Alert observation is crucial for learning in a movement discipline such as ballet, where exercises and patterns typically are demonstrated by the instructor for the students to follow. The ability to imitate a movement phrase is important in the highly competitive professional dance world, a world that is virtually closed to those who cannot quickly and correctly reproduce a given movement pattern. For professional and amateur alike, correct performance of a movement helps prevent injury. Although the mind cannot control specific muscles, if it correctly understands the idea of a movement, then correct muscles will function when the movement is executed. Correct execution cannot always be achieved simply by unthinkingly copying another's movement pattern. Be open to suggestions; be willing to try new ways of learning; be not afraid to ask questions.

Remember that the face is part of the dance image. Agnes de Mille, choreographer and wise and witty author, has these words of advice for the dance student: "Do not grimace while you practice. Learn to make all the necessary effort with a quiet, controlled face—a quiet face, mark you, not a dull face."[1]

A modicum of good manners is expected in the classroom. For instance, when a progression of movement is to begin from one side of the studio, a slow saunter to the designated area is no more appropriate than a fast sprint to the front of the line. In classes in which there are students of several levels of technique, common protocol is for the more advanced dancers to stand in the front line or to lead off in a combination. In a class of all beginners, it is both wise and courteous to be ready to move to the front but not to expect always to be there. Be aware that everyone in class needs space in which to move. Learning to move while keeping a certain distance from and a certain relationship to other dancers is one of the challenges and rewards of dance study.

If students stop work more than momentarily in a class, they should not start again during that class period. Injuries can occur when cooled muscles are suddenly asked to work vigorously. Similarly, latecomers should not expect to take class if the first exercises have been missed. Dance study is a cumulative experience, each lesson building on the one before, just as the exercises of each lesson build on one another.

Again to quote Miss de Mille: "Remember always that the point of every exercise is to strengthen and soften, that the object is not how high, how fast, or how long, but how harmonious and how lovely. Do the exercises slowly and carefully at first. Forget speed. Speed will take care of itself later."[2]

## THE MUSIC

The integral relationship of ballet and music is nicely summed up by choreographer and teacher George Balanchine as he described his collaboration with composer Igor Stravinsky: "His music provides the dancer's floor. It's the reason for us to move. Without the music we don't want to move."[3]

Prior to the twentieth century, the ballet teacher was also the accompanist for his own classes, playing a small violin as his students performed their exercises and combinations. Today, the piano is the classroom instrument, and the piano accompanist is a vital component of every class. When a good accompanist is not available, a teacher may use records, perhaps those made especially for ballet classes, with appropriate bands for different exercises.

Music is selected from a variety of sources: piano pieces from nineteenth-century composers such as Franz Schubert and Frédéric Chopin, as well as piano adaptations from ballet scores. Leo Delibes, Mikhail Glinka, and Peter I. Tchaikovsky are among those whose music is especially suitable, but twentieth-century marches, rags, and show tunes can provide appropriate accompaniment for certain movements, as can compositions from later composers such as Francis Poulenc and Sergei Prokofiev.

Knowledge of music is useful for the study of ballet. Even students who have not studied music will soon learn to count it; that is, they will hear the musical beat or pulse and will recognize a few fundamental musical rhythms and be able to keep time with them.

During ballet classes, the instructor probably will demonstrate an exercise and then count it: *1 and 2 and 3 and 4.* . . . The numbers are the *beats*, with number 1 having the heaviest beat, or accent. Those four beats make a certain kind of *rhythm* called a 4/4 rhythm (or meter). Series of counts repeated over and over are called *bars* or *measures*. A series of measures is called a *phrase*.

Below are listed the musical rhythms that are used most often in beginning ballet classes. They are divided into measures, as indicated by the / mark. The heavy accent of each rhythm is indicated by underlining the number; the lighter accent, by the symbol ´. Each example is four bars long. Count these rhythms out loud; then try clapping or walking to them, accenting the first count of each measure:

2/4:  1̲ 2 / 1̲ 2 / 1̲ 2 / 1̲ 2 /
4/4:  1̲ 2 3́ 4 / 1̲ 2 3́ 4 / 1̲ 2 3́ 4 / 1̲ 2 3́ 4 /
3/4:  1̲ 2 3 / 1̲ 2 3 / 1̲ 2 3 / 1̲ 2 3 /
6/8:  1̲ 2 3 4́ 5 6 / 1̲ 2 3 4́ 5 6 / 1̲ 2 3 4́ 5 6 / 1̲ 2 3 4́ 5 6 /

The speed (*tempo*) of these rhythms can vary from fast (*allegro*) to slow (*adagio*). Dance movements use these same terms: fast steps are called *allegro*; slow, sustained movements are called *adagio* (or the French form, *adage*).

Ballet exercises are usually done an even number of times; that is, a step is repeated four or eight or sixteen times. (Sometimes a step may be done three times with a hold or pause in place of the fourth step.) Similarly, combinations of steps usually are done four or eight times. This is in contrast to modern dance exercises, which often are done an odd number of times (three, five, seven . . .). Moreover, modern dancers frequently use many different rhythms for one dance phrase (such as 1̲ 2 3 / 1̲ 2 3́ 4 / 1̲ 2 / 1̲ 2 3́ 4 . . .). Rarely does a ballet teacher experiment in these ways, although occasionally such experiments may be rewarding, especially when working with an accompanist who is adept at improvising.

There are times when a ballet exercise or combination of steps will be learned first in one rhythm, such as 2/4, then tried in another rhythm, such as 6/8. The steps will look and feel slightly different when such a change is made. A change in *tempo* will have an effect also; for example, a faster tempo requires smaller movements covering less space.

To help students know when to be ready to begin an exercise, the accompanist will play a few notes of introduction, which the teacher may count aloud. "Tune in" to these cues and be prepared to move at the designated time, not several beats later.

*Beat, rhythm, bar, phrase, tempo*—all may seem bewildering to the beginner. A teacher recognizes this and will try to help. For instance, a particular exercise for the leg may be demonstrated and then described by the teacher as "point, lift, point, close." The teacher may then count the exercise as "one, two, three, four." The music will play the same rhythm. Very soon the student will see, hear, and feel that rhythm as 4/4. And in time, the student will become equally acquainted with other musical forms, such as the waltz (3/4, with the accent on the first beat), the polka (2/4), and the mazurka (also 3/4, but with the accent on the second beat).

Although responding to the musical beat is fundamental to dance, the classroom would be dull indeed if the musical accompaniment offered merely a flat, steady rhythm. Students' ears should be trained along with their muscles. Phrases of movement and music are the goal—not just steps or notes.

## THE VOCABULARY

Because ballet was first nurtured in the royal courts and academies of France, French became the language of the art. All ballet exercises, steps, body positions, and movement directions have French names. These names are in use in every ballet studio the world over, although such wide diffusion has led to certain differences, even corruption in specific terminology.

It is advantageous to have studied French, but students who have not will soon have a number of French words in their vocabulary after a few classes in ballet. When understood, these words can greatly simplify directions that a teacher might otherwise have to use. In addition, the terminology simplifies the task of writing down class work or choreography, should that sometime be necessary or desirable.

## STYLE

As might be expected, such a global art includes some regional differences in training and in the manner in which steps and poses are executed—differences in style. Briefly described, the French have emphasized charm and elegance, whereas the Italian school has stressed technical virtuosity. The Russian school was founded by French ballet masters, but later it adopted and adapted the more brilliant technique of the Italians. The combination of these and other sources produced the strength and flair characteristic of Russian dancers. In contrast, the British style is less flamboyant, more serene. The Danish school has maintained the exuberant lightness and speed of its French-trained nineteenth-century mentor, August Bournonville. The methods of two outstanding teachers, Enrico Cecchetti (1850–1928) and Agrippina Vaganova (1879–1951), have created methods of technique now being handed down by their many pupils. And, there is an American style, a blend of French, Italian, and Russian influences with a distinctive dose of American restless energy and youthful spirit. The style of a class will reflect one of these or other schools, depending on the training of the teacher.

This book is offered as a general ballet text, rather than a presentation of one particular instructional method. It does, however, reflect much of the author's

training with Margaret Craske and Dolores Mitrovich in the Cecchetti Method
and with Thalia Mara and Arthur Mahoney of the National Academy of Ballet.

11
THE BALLET CLASS

## THE LESSON

A first lesson in ballet may seem more like a class in basic anatomy than a
dancing class. But, without an understanding of proper body alignment and
placement, there can be no progress in work toward balance and form, with
freedom and economy of movement. In addition, the very exercises that lead to
control, strength, and beauty of line in ballet can also lead to weaknesses and
injuries when attempted by a poorly aligned body.

## Alignment

*Alignment* in ballet essentially means good posture; that is, the various body
parts — head, shoulders, arms, ribs, hips, legs, feet — are in correct relative position with one another. Bad posture can result in a slump, with rounded shoulders and droopy head, or a sway, with the pelvis tilted forward, causing a hollow
look to the lower back. These distortions in alignment are detrimental enough

Good posture                                    Poor posture to an ordinary body, but they can be positively hazardous for the ballet student. In his book *Dancing Without Danger*, Donald F. Featherstone warns of the cumulative effect of poor alignment: "Any departure from the balanced posture will strain muscles and ligaments and cause undue friction in joints — if one segment of the body is out of line, all others will be affected."[4]

Ballet *placement* refers to a well-aligned body that is shifted slightly forward from the ankle over the ball of the foot. Thus, when standing with the legs parallel and the focus straight ahead, a direct vertical line could be drawn from between the eyes, down through the navel to the tips of the toes. A dancer is said to be "placed" when the muscles of the body have become educated to assume such a position of correct alignment without effort. Once achieved, good posture requires less effort to maintain than poor posture. Correct placement is a slow process, however, requiring many classes, often many years of work. In ballet the body is always active, not static, thus requiring a dynamic, yet subtle "realigning" as it assumes new and different poses.

Some dancers and ballet teachers use specific anatomical terminology, whereas others use more general language to convey the fundamentals of correct alignment necessary for ballet. It is helpful to contemplate these fundamentals one at a time, keeping in mind that the goal is to find the most efficient posture for the work ahead.

**The Feet**  To begin an understanding of proper alignment and placement for ballet, stand with the feet a few inches apart, pointing straight ahead. The feet should feel relaxed, the toes flat, with the weight of the body resting mainly on three points: the heel, the base of the big toe, and the little toe. In this position, as in the ballet positions discussed later, the arch of the foot is supported, the ankles are prevented from rolling inward or outward, and the body is given a strong base from which to work.

**The Legs**  Straighten the knees firmly, *but do not push them back*; they should be directly over the feet. Now bend the knees, keeping the heels on the floor, and check to see that the knees are pointing directly over the front of the feet. This knee-over-foot alignment is correct for any bend of the knees, whether in this parallel position or in the turned-out positions of ballet. Begin to straighten the knees and also begin to sense a lengthening of the thighs.

**The Torso**  The pelvis should be in a midway position, neither tucking under nor sticking out. To check this position, place the palm of one hand on the abdomen (which ought to feel flat and compressed) and the back of the other hand on the lower spine (the "small of the back"). The front hand should be perpendicular to the floor and the back hand nearly so. The natural curves of the spine, which allow it to be flexible and to absorb shock, must be neither exaggerated nor entirely flattened out. Maintaining a firm abdomen and an extended spine will help achieve correct alignment in a more efficient way than the oft-misunderstood admonition to "tuck under your hips."

The rib cage should be directly in line with the hips. At no time should the rib cage feel rigid or forced forward; breathing should remain normal.

To feel the correct position of shoulders, lift them up toward the ears, hold them there a few seconds, and then let them drop. Now feel the shoulder blades resting downward. The shoulders will be low but not pulled backward. Let the arms hang naturally from this position with the hands relaxed (shake them first to relieve any tension), the fingers and thumbs separated naturally.

**The Head**   The head must be in alignment with the ribs and hips. The back of the neck is kept long, for it is a continuation of the spine, on which the head lightly rests. The chin is parallel to the floor, but never thrust forward. The eyes look forward, not down.

**Other Methods**   It is not unusual to find lessons in body alignment occurring with students not standing, as described above, but lying on the floor. New approaches to understanding movement—changing habitual muscle and neurological patterns, releasing tensions, conditioning and strengthening the body, as well as achieving more efficient posture—are some of the goals of today's many body therapy methods. Pioneers in the development of these methods include Dr. Lulu E. Sweigard, Frederick M. Alexander, Irmgard Bartenieff, Moshe Feldenkrais, and Joseph Pilates. (For further discussion, see Chapter 5, "Body Therapies and Conditioning Methods.") Such body therapy methods are being integrated into the work of some dancers and instructors as they seek new and more appropriate ways of performing, teaching, and, not least, aligning the bones of the body.

## Turnout

The student must also deal with another essential element related to alignment: the turnout of the legs at the hip joints. The legs are rotated outward from that joint *only as far as that position can be maintained by the rotator muscles around the hip joint, without disturbing body alignment.* Ideally, this turnout is 180 degrees, but it is very seldom realistic for most beginning students (children or adults). Individual differences in body structure and strength should determine the degree of turnout. Whatever that degree, the arches of the feet must remain lifted and the ankles straight. Remember that the weight of the body rests on the base of the big and little toes and the heel. As discussed in the preceding section, correct ballet placement requires the weight to be shifted slightly forward from the ankle so that it rests more on the balls of the feet than back on the heels. In maintaining this position it is important that the pelvis not tilt forward nor the buttocks tuck under. The knees should always be in line with the feet, following the same rule of alignment as in the parallel position: When the knees are bent, they ought to be over the center of the feet.

Although this position may feel strange at first, it is important to understand that the turnout of the legs in ballet is merely an exaggeration of a perfectly normal action for the human body. The top of the thigh bone can rotate either inward or outward in the hip socket. Ballet technique simply has capitalized on the outward rotation possibility. In maintaining the turnout, there should be no

Realistic turnout for
many beginners

sense of strain or tension. The body must not be stiff and locked in position. It must be firm, yet at ease and free to move.

Historically, complete turnout developed slowly—by 1700 the angle of turnout was 90 degrees; by 1800 it was 180 degrees. A similar progression is mirrored in a student's training; a beginner works from positions of lesser turnout, advancing gradually as the body learns to maintain correct alignment in the more extreme positions. This must be a slow and careful process.

## THE FIVE POSITIONS OF THE FEET

The five positions of the feet, codified in the late-seventeenth century, are the foundations of ballet technique. (See Chapter 7, "Birth of the Classical Ballet," for the historical context.) Every ballet step, movement, and pose relate in some way to one or more of these positions. In all five positions, the weight must be equally distributed on both feet, the legs straight unless purposefully flexed. The hips remain squared to the front, the pelvis in its upright position, and the legs turned out from the hip joints. The ideal positions (that is, with complete 180-degree turnout) are illustrated and described here.

> First position: the legs turned out from the hips, the heels and knees touching, the feet forming a straight line
>
> Second position: the legs turned out from the hips, as in first position, but the heels separated and directly under the shoulders
>
> Third position: the legs turned out from the hips, one foot directly in front of the other, with the heel of each foot touching the middle of the other foot
>
> Fourth position: the legs turned out from the hips, one foot directly forward of the other and one footlength apart (for crossed fourth position) or forward the same distance from first position (for open fourth position)

| First | Second | Third | Fourth crossed | Fourth open | Fifth |

Fifth position: the legs turned out from the hips, one foot directly in front of the other, with the heel of the front foot at the joint of the toe of the back foot

At the beginning of training it is wise to begin and end exercises in first position; later exercises can be done from third, and finally from the more demanding fifth position.

## POSITIONS OF THE ARMS

The positions of the arms correspond to the positions of the feet. However, no rule says that if the feet are in fifth position, the arms must always be in a particular position. Some variation occurs in the numbering and naming of the basic arm positions in different teaching methods. It is pointless to argue over numbers or names; learn those used in your school and concentrate on the desired shape of the arms. Although there are slight variations in the style of the positions, the following general rules of form can be helpful for most basic positions: The arms curve gently from shoulder to fingertip, eliminating the pointed look of the elbows. The hands are held simply, the wrists neither stiff nor floppy, the fingers curved and only slightly separated, with the thumb and middle finger brought relatively close together. In midlevel positions, either to the front or to the side, the arms may have a gradual slope downward from the shoulders to the elbows, then to the wrists, and finally to the fingers. The arms should move freely from the shoulder sockets so as not to raise or pull the shoulders. When the hand is over the head, it should be just within the line of vision as the performer looks straight forward.

The following descriptions and illustrations represent only one of several possibilities for terminology, style, and numbering of arm positions; others are equally valid.

Basic positions in which the arms and hands are to the side of the body and, usually, just slightly forward:

■ First (preparatory)     ■ *Demi-seconde*                    ■ Second

Basic positions in which the hands are centered on the body, only a few inches apart, the arms forming an oval shape:

■ *Bras bas (en bas)*
(arms low)

■ *Bras avant (en avant)*
(arms forward)

■ *Bras hauts (en haut)*
(arms high)

Possible variations of these basic positions, which have a variety of different names and numbers, include:

## POSITIONS OF THE HEAD

During *barre* work in beginning classes, the position of the head seldom varies. It is held regally on a long neck, with chin parallel to the floor and eyes looking (not staring) straight forward. This attitude sets the tone for the elegant style of ballet, but in center work the head must learn to move in harmony with the rest of the body. Five different positions of the head can be used:

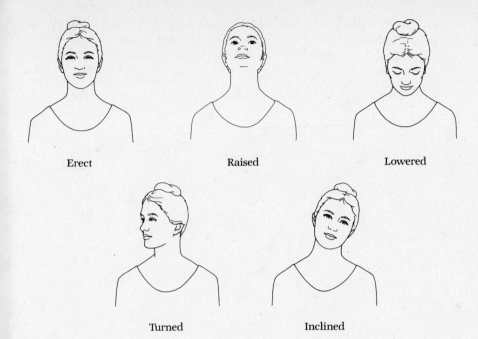

Erect            Raised            Lowered

Turned            Inclined

These positions can be combined, for instance:

Turned and inclined        Lowered and turned

## SPECIAL CONSIDERATIONS
### Balancing on One Leg

As already mentioned, a dancer's body is expected to be centered, the weight of the body resting evenly on both feet while imaginary lines dissect the body vertically from head to toe and horizontally across the body at hip level. A shift of weight to one foot, with the other leg extended or raised, brings a challenge to this sense of center. The vertical center line moves, from the supporting ankle up through the top of the body, until it is in line with the center of the supporting foot. Turnout on the supporting leg is maintained through control of the rotator muscles around the hip joint. A horizontal line must be maintained across the hips, avoiding any tendency to "sit" into the supporting leg or to raise the other hip.

Properly balanced                                    Improperly balanced

## Balancing on the Ball of the Foot

All five positions of the feet can be done with the heels raised and the weight on the balls of the feet. In beginning work these are done to quarter point and half point; after sufficient strength is acquired they can be done to three-quarter point. Many steps and poses are taken in these raised positions.

Quarter point     Half point     Three-quarter point

Practice

Stand with the feet parallel. Lift one heel as high as possible (allowing the knee to bend) while keeping the ball of that foot firmly on the floor. The ankle and knee should be in line with the big toe and the second toe. Now try practicing this position with the legs turned out. If the foot leans toward only the big toe or toward the little toe, it is said to be "sickled," a potentially harmful position for the ankles and knees, as well as the feet, especially when landing from aerial movements. Landing with the feet poorly aligned can result in sprains and even breaks.

## Pointing the Foot

When pointing the foot, the foot extends from the ankle joint through the longitudinal and metatarsal arches to the toes. The toes compress together in a stretched, rather than a curled or knuckled-under, position. The center of the foot and the toes form a direct line with the ankle.

Correctly          Incorrectly
pointed foot      pointed foot

### Practice

Sit on the floor, or well back in a chair, legs together and straight, the feet flexed (bent) at the ankles. Slowly begin arching the feet, working inch-by-inch from the ankle through the insteps of the feet to the balls of the feet, and then to the toes. The knees should remain straight. The toes should appear as a continuation of the arch of the pointed foot, creating a smooth line with the leg. The toes are pressed together but not "knuckled under."

## Warm-Up

Dancers frequently like to limber their bodies gently before the actual class begins. This warm-up can help awaken the muscles, as well as the mind, for the work ahead by raising the body temperature and increasing the supply of blood.

Some teachers may even begin the lesson with such preparatory exercises, not leaving it to beginners to warm up on their own. Following are examples of simple movements that may be used as a warm-up. Note that these are done slowly and without jumps or extreme stretches; gradually, over time, increase the number of repetitions.

### Practice

To warm the neck area: Bend the head forward, then lift the face toward the ceiling; tilt the head from side to side; turn the head from side to side; roll the head in a circle.

To warm the chest area: Lift the shoulders toward the ears, let them drop; circle the shoulders; circle the arms forward, up, and back.

To stretch out the entire body: Reach upward, sideward, and forward.

To activate the reflexes: Bend slowly forward, starting with the head and "rolling" down through each vertebra of the spine. "Hang" in this forward position with the body relaxed, the knees slightly bent. Reverse the movements, returning to an upright position with the body in correct alignment. Do this in parallel position, then in first position.

To warm the ankles and feet: Circle the foot at the ankle; flex and point the foot (as described above). Lift the heel of one foot while pressing the ball of that foot on the floor; complete the arching of the foot by pointing through the toes and allowing them to leave the floor slightly; reverse the action by rolling down through the toes to the ball of the foot, then lowering the heel.

To warm up the hip joint: Lift the knee several times to the front; gently swing the leg forward and backward.

To warm the calf muscles: Face the *barre* with legs parallel and the feet a few inches apart; lean into the *barre*, keeping the legs straight and the heels firmly on the floor; hold this position and then return to the original stance.

To strengthen the abdominal muscles while lying on the back, knees bent and the soles of the feet on the floor: Clasp the hands in front of the body and reach forward between the knees, raising first the head, then the shoulders and upper back off the floor; keep the waist pressed to the floor and the stomach flat; slowly return to the original position by reversing the action.

## Correct Breathing

The ultimate skill that every dancer strives for is to work with concentration and calm control of the body, but without tension. To achieve this, the breath is instrumental. . . . Ballet dancing, which seems to mask ordinary human function, achieves its characteristic lightness and elegance with the use of breath. The inhaled breath can literally lift you up in the air as you jump or are raised by a partner. . . . All movement must have breath and flow; otherwise it looks flat and lifeless.[5]

This means deep or diaphragmatic breathing, in which air is inhaled, filling the middle and lower lungs, as the rib cage and the spine lift. The arms can reflect this expansion by slightly opening and rising to the sides during inhalation, then returning gently as the breath is exhaled. This natural action is fundamental to the movement of the arms (called *port de bras* in ballet); when the body rises onto the toes or into the air during steps or springs, it will inhale naturally, and the arms will naturally want to lift also. As the body returns to the ground, the breath will be exhaled, and the arms will lower. Breathing during exercises will not be in a constant, even rhythm, however. The body will naturally want to inhale longer or more quickly, depending on the difficulty of an exercise.

Shallow breathing (where only the upper, smaller part of the lung is used) does not give the dancer enough oxygen. Yawns during a class can indicate lack of oxygen rather than lack of interest. Raoul Gelabert, dance therapist, suggests the following exercise to develop deeper breathing:

> Stand, arms at the side, and breathe in through the nose, filling the abdomen with one deep breath. Holding the breath, bend forward, allowing the spine to curve, sharply contract and exhale the air through the mouth. With the abdomen completely empty of air, return to the upright position. Repeat.[6]

The releasing of muscular tension by this exercise also contributes to a gentle stretch, sensed especially in the lower back and down the legs.

## Learning

People learn at different speeds and in very individual ways. A beginning ballet class challenges "traditional" learning habits because it engages a multiplicity of sensory, kinesthetic, and mental channels. Eyes must catch the visual image demonstrated; ears must tune into the rhythmic and harmonic patterns of the music; the mind must analyze complex movement details. Sometimes muscles respond and remember before the conscious mind does.

Technical progress usually occurs in a stair-step fashion, rather than in a smooth, continuously ascending line. Thus, technical plateaus—periods seeming without change (that is, improvement)—are inevitable. And then, a glorious breakthrough will occur, and another stair step has been climbed. That is the time to congratulate oneself and enjoy the pleasures of accomplishment. Then, once more, have the discipline to continue, for the key to progress is regular class attendance and consistent work—mind and senses and muscles fully involved.

**NOTES**

1. Agnes de Mille, *To a Young Dancer* (Boston: Little, Brown, 1960), 24.

2. *Ibid.*

3. Quoted in Selma Jeanne Cohen, *Dance as a Theatre Art* (New York: Harper & Row, 1974), 190.

4. Donald F. Featherstone, *Dancing Without Danger* (South Brunswick and New York: Barnes, 1970), 65.

5. Ellen Jacob, *Dancing, A Guide to the Dancer You Can Be* (Reading, Mass.: Addison-Wesley, 1981), 210.

6. Raoul Gelabert, *Anatomy for the Dancer*, vol. 2 (New York: Dance Magazine, 1966), 55.

# CHAPTER 2
# BALLET TECHNIQUE: *BARRE* WORK

The first formal segment of classroom instruction begins with exercises done at the *barre*. Although each exercise has its own purpose, *barre* work as a whole is designed to strengthen the feet, legs, and back; to increase range of movement (especially at the hip); to attain balance and control; to stabilize turnout; and to gain speed in the feet and lightness in the legs—in other words, to instill the "mechanics" of ballet technique.

## USE OF THE *BARRE*

The *barre* itself is meant as a hand support only, steadying the body but not bearing its weight. In the early stages of training, while doing many exercises, the student faces the *barre* with both hands resting lightly on it, close together, and the elbows relaxed and slightly bent. This position gives the beginner an extra aid in centering the body because the hips and shoulders can be kept parallel with the horizontal line of the *barre*. Later, most exercises are done with the body sideways to the *barre*, one hand on the *barre* somewhat forward of the shoulder, the fingers resting on top of the *barre* with the thumb along the side of the *barre* rather than below it. The body should be far enough from the *barre* to allow the elbow to be relaxed and slightly bent.

Before an exercise begins, the free arm "prepares" by rising forward to the level of the fork in the ribs and then opening out to the side, where it usually remains throughout the exercise. The leg farther from the *barre* (the "outside" leg) typically is the gesture leg of the exercise. Because exercises traditionally begin with the right leg, the dancer begins with the left hand on the *barre*. To help avoid a certain "right-leggedness" in dancers, it is wise to begin exercises occasionally on the other side. Sometimes, too, it is helpful to "prepare" with both arms, raising them forward so that the hands are centered on the torso, opening them outward to the side, and then taking the *barre* with the inside hand. When an exercise is completed, both arms are lowered, and the final position is held momentarily before turning to repeat the exercise with the other leg.

Beginners may spend most of their early classes at the *barre*, with the time being gradually reduced to about one-half of the period, but never to less than one-third. The length of an entire class is commonly one and a half hours, although scheduling patterns in colleges and universities sometimes necessitate shorter sessions.

## SEQUENCE OF EXERCISES

No universally accepted order of sequence for *barre* exercises exists, but in most classes work at *barre* begins with the most basic movement of ballet, the *plié*, or bend of the legs, and finishes with the vigorous movements of *grand battement*, or large beating action of the leg. Although the sequence varies somewhat from teacher to teacher and from school to school, in general the smaller, slower movements are done first, legs are gradually warmed up from the feet to the knees to the hips, and combinations of movements grow from simple to more complex. The *barre* exercises discussed in the following pages are arranged in broad general categories that do not reflect any preferred order of teaching. Because they lay the foundation for the entire technique of ballet, they will be described in some detail, the three most fundamental exercises deserving first attention. But it must be remembered that the most specific instructions, cautions, or hints from a printed page cannot *teach* the mechanics and artistry of ballet even to the most willing student. Neither can the finest illustrations. Therefore, this is not intended as a how-to-do-it section, but rather as a resource for, and supplement to, classroom study.

## THREE FUNDAMENTAL EXERCISES: *PLIÉ, ÉLEVÉ/RELEVÉ, AND BATTEMENT TENDU*

The following three exercises represent ballet's most fundamental movements of the legs—bending and straightening the knees, raising and lowering the heels, and stretching the foot along the floor to a pointed position before returning it to a closed position.

### *Plié* (plee-AY)
**Definition**  A *plié* is a bending movement of the legs, beginning at the top of the thighs, through the knees and into the ankles. A half-bend is called a *demi-plié (d'mee-plee-AY)*; a deep bend, a *grand plié* (grahn plee-AY). (Technically, a bend on only one leg is not a *plié* but a *fondu*.)

**Purpose**   Almost every step in ballet—certainly every jumping movement—involves a bending movement of the legs. The correct execution of the *demi-plié* (and the *fondu*) gives a springy quality to steps of elevation and a lightness to all dance movements. The *grand plié* is important in stretching and strengthening the legs because the entire weight of the upper body is lowered and raised by the legs. Both *demi-plié* and *grand plié* require even distribution of the weight on both feet, thus making it easier to center the body and to master the turnout of the legs. Both types of *plié* increase the circulation of the blood in the legs, thus facilitating warm-up. Knowing how and when to bend and straighten the knees is the cornerstone of ballet technique.

**Description**   *Pliés* are done in all positions of the feet. During the *demi-plié*, the heels never leave the floor. The movement begins in the high, inner side of the thighs; the knees open outward in a direct line over the toes until the depth of the *demi-plié* is reached (determined by the length of the Achilles tendon connecting the calf muscle and the heel); then the legs return to their original straight position.

■ *Demi-plié* in first position

Balanced, smooth motion

The *grand plié* begins exactly as the *demi-plié*, but when the maximum stretch of the Achilles tendon is felt, the heels are allowed to release from the floor and the knees continue to bend over the feet until, ideally, the thighs are almost parallel with the floor. Immediately the action is reversed: The heels press into the floor, the knees straighten, and the thighs continue to lengthen upward until the original position is attained. The *grand plié* thus described is done in all positions except the second and the open fourth positions, where, because of the spread of the legs, the heels need not and should not be released from the floor.

**Reminders**   In all *pliés*, the body must be centered over the feet, the spine must remain erect, with the pelvis in the midway position—that is, neither

■ *Grand plié* in first position

A two-way motion: the spine lengthening upward as the body descends then reaching
downward on the return to the original position

■ *Demi-plié* and *grand plié* in second position

Thighs, rotating sideward as well as lowering downward

pushed forward nor released backward. The feet must be securely placed on the
floor but not tense, with the arches supported so they do not roll. The correct
alignment of the ankles should be maintained without tension at the depth of
the *demi-plié*. The weight of the body must not settle into the knees at the depth
of the *grand plié*. The movement of the *plié* should be smooth and slow but
without pauses at any point in the exercise. The straightening of the legs must
be done as carefully as the bending of them. When the legs are crossed, as in
third, fourth, and fifth positions, it is important that the weight continue to be
distributed evenly on both feet (the temptation often is to lean toward the back

■ **Incorrect** *pliés*

| Arches rolling and knees forward | Weight settled into knees | Pelvis released backward |

foot). These crossed positions also require great care in opening the knees equally, so that one knee lowers to the same level as the other (the tendency often is to drop the back knee, especially in the fourth position). The depth of the *grand plié* is determined by the strength of the muscles on the inner side of the thighs and by the length of the Achilles tendon. Therefore, the thighs ought not to be lowered all the way to the horizontal position unless correct body alignment can be maintained throughout the *plié*.

**Suggestions**   Learn to execute the *demi-plié* correctly before attempting the *grand plié*. Begin the study of *pliés* in the first and second positions; later add the third position and when sufficient strength has developed, the fourth and fifth positions (when changing to a new position, move only one foot and do not look at it). Learn the *pliés* facing the *barre* before trying them sideways or with movements of the arm.

Because *grand pliés* are an especially strenuous exercise for the knees, they should be limited in number and performed after the legs are warmed up. Thus, while *demi-pliés* are appropriate as a first exercise, *grands pliés* may be more safely and effectively performed later in the *barre* sequence.

### *Élevé* (el-e-VAY)/*Relevé* (ruhl-e-VAY)

**Definition**   An *élevé* is a rise from straight legs to the balls of the feet, the *demi-pointes* (d'mee-PWAHNT). When the rise is made from a preceding *demi-plié*, it is called *relevé*, meaning raised or relifted.

**Purpose**   Strength, suppleness, and control of the feet are developed by both the *élevé* and the *relevé*. As the thighs lengthen upward during the rise, the knees and the muscles of the legs are strengthened also, building a strong, secure position on *demi-pointes*, so important for balance, turns, and many steps of ballet, including those later done on full point by advanced students (traditionally, women only). Because it combines both a bend and rise, the *relevé* serves also as a preparatory exercise for jumps.

**Description**   *Élevés* and *relevés* are done in all positions of the feet. In the simpler movement, the *élevé*, the heels and legs stretch upward from the floor as the body rises to the *demi-pointes*. As the heels press downward in the return to the floor, the legs continue to lengthen as the body returns to its original position without a bend of the knees. Although *demi-pointe* literally means half-point, the term often is used for any of three levels—quarter, half, and three-quarter—which denote the relative distance of the heels from the floor. (See Chapter 1, "Balancing on the Ball of the Foot.")

■  *Relevé* to three-quarter point

Verticality with strong upward thrust

The *relevé* is preceded and followed by a *demi-plié*, therefore requiring a high degree of coordination: The push of the heels from the floor must be properly timed with the straightening of the knees and lengthening upward of the thighs; the lowering of the heels to the floor and the bending of the legs must be carefully controlled but without tension.

The action can be smooth, with the heels raised and lowered in the same spot, or the action can be quick and springy, with a firm push against the floor that pulls the toes underneath the ankles in the *demi-pointe* position. Two basic *relevés* of the latter type are the *sous-sus* and the *échappé*. The *sous-sus* (soo-siu) is a *relevé* made with a slight spring allowing the feet to slide together from fifth position *demi-plié* to a tight fifth position on *demi-pointes*, the feet moving equally toward the center of the body. The *échappé* (ay-shah-PAY) is a *relevé* made with a slight spring allowing the feet to slide apart from fifth position

■ *Sous-sus*  ■ *Échappé relevé*

Connecting the preparatory *demi-plié* with the light spring to the *demi-pointes*

*demi-plié* to an open position on *demi-pointes* (to second position; later to fourth), the feet moving equally from the center of the body. After both types of springing *relevés*, the feet return to their original position in *demi-plié*, also by means of a slight spring.

**Reminders**  In all *demi-pointes* positions on two feet, the body must be centered over both feet. The turnout of the legs must be maintained throughout the raising and lowering of the heels. The body should be lengthened as much as possible so that the weight rests lightly on the balls of the feet, toward the first three toes (beginners should never rise to the full point; this is done only by advanced women students who wear shoes specially constructed for work on full point). The feet must never be allowed to roll either in or out because that weakens the ankles and the arches of the feet. The knees must be straight in *demi-pointes* positions.

**Suggestions**  Learn the *élevé* in first and second positions; later practice it in the other positions of the feet. When the principles of *élevé* have been mastered, add the *relevés*, beginning with those requiring slow, smooth action. Later try the springing *relevés*. The exercises first should be practiced facing the *barre*.

**Related Exercises**  *Relevés* also can be taken to only one foot following a *demi-plié* from any of the five positions of the feet or from a position in *fondu*. The raised foot, well pointed and turned out, usually is brought in front or in back of the supporting ankle or knee. From there it can return to a *demi-plié* position, or it can remain lifted while the supporting foot lowers into a *fondu* position.

A *demi-détourné* (d'mee-day-toor-NAY) is useful in making a half-turn pivot to face the other direction at the *barre*, thus changing sides for an exercise. Following a *sous-sus*, make a half-turn pivot toward the back foot. The feet thus change relationship—the foot that was behind now is in front. Both heels then lower on completion of the *demi-détourné*.

### *Battement Tendu* (baht-MAH*n* tah*n*-DIU)

**Definition**   Literally, *battement* means "beating." In ballet the term refers to almost every leg movement at the *barre*. There are over twenty types of *battements*, but the most fundamental is the *battement tendu*, often simply called tendu ("stretched"). In this exercise, the gesture foot, starting from a closed position, is extended along the floor until it is fully arched and the toes pointed; then it is returned to a closed position at the supporting leg.

**Purpose**   More than any exercise, the *battement tendu* strengthens the foot by alternating the tension of arching and pointing the foot with the relaxation of the toes and then the arch as the foot returns along the floor. The *tendu* is basic to many other exercises and steps of ballet, and, as typically the first exercise done with one leg at the *barre*, it is basic to the centering of the body on the supporting leg.

**Description**   In *battements tendus*, the toes never leave the floor. The movement is initiated at the top of the leg; turnout is controlled through use of the rotator and accessory muscles around the hip joint as the foot slides outward from a closed position (first, third, or fifth) until the heel has to be raised in order not to shift the center of the body away from the supporting leg. Immediately the foot begins to arch, first through the instep and then through the ball of the foot until the maximum stretch of the *tendu* is reached. To return to the closed position, first the ball of the foot relaxes and then the instep, until all tension is released and the heel is placed firmly on the floor, the thighs drawn together and the weight again centered over both feet. Both legs remain straight throughout the exercise.

Tendus are done to the front, to the side, and to the back. When an exercise is done consecutively to these directions, it is said to be done *en croix* (ahn krwah) — in the shape of a cross. When the tips of the toes touch the floor, foot fully arched and knee straight, the position is termed *pointe tendue* (pwahnt tah*n*-DIU) — "point stretched."

■ *Battement tendu à la seconde*

Stretching and elongating the leg and foot outward — then reversing the direction to
return with a strong close

**Reminders**  Correct body alignment must be maintained, special care being taken not to "sit" into the supporting hip. Turnout of the supporting leg and foot is essential so that the hip does not release and the foot does not roll. Weight should never shift to the extended foot, thus putting pressure on the pointed toes. The knee of the gesture leg should remain straight as the leg opens and closes. Proper alignment of the heel and the toes is maintained by keeping the heel forward, which also helps assure the turned out shape of the leg.

**Suggestions**  In *battements tendus* to the side, the movement of the foot should travel along a path indicated by the degree of turnout, maintained by the strength of the rotators and accessory muscles around the hip joint. The direction of the path will therefore be one's own position *à la seconde* rather than directly "to the side."

In *battements tendus* to the front (*à la quatrième devant*), the heel leads the way forward so that the bone at the inside of the ankle remains forward as much as possible. As the foot returns, the toes lead the way to the closed position, and the inside ankle bone remains forward. In this way, correct alignment is maintained, and the foot does not "sickle."

■ *Battement tendu à la quatrième devant*

Inside of the ankle reaching forward

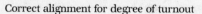

Correct alignment for degree of turnout      **Incorrect** alignment      **Incorrect** or "sickled" position

Energy flowing upward as foot extends backward

**Incorrect** *battement* alignment

The process is reversed for *battements tendus* to the back (*à la quatrième derrière*): The toes lead the way backward, the heel leads the way for the return, with the bone at the outside of the ankle pointing backward as much as possible throughout the exercise. A lengthening of the torso upward with some shift of the body weight forward will help accommodate the slight forward tilt of the pelvis in *tendus* to the back. In *battements tendus* to the front or side, the foot should point to the tip of the big toe (and often of the second toe as well). However, when performed to the back, the point is to the tip of the *side* of the big toe.

Begin the study of this exercise by stretching the foot *à la seconde* from first position, later from third position (better to use a good third than a poor fifth position), closing in front each time for a series of *battements*, then closing in back each time. Later the closings can alternate front and back of the supporting foot and to *demi-plié* as well as the straight position.

*Battements tendus* forward or backward are best learned from third position (and later practiced from fifth position) rather than first position because the point of the foot in line with the crossed position gives a clearer concept of the basic front direction (*quatrième devant*) and back direction (*quatrième derrière*). Artistic preference and individual body construction will determine whether the toes of the extended foot are directly in line with the center of the body or more in line with the heel of the supporting foot.

In a beginning class, *battements* should first be practiced slowly and evenly without frequent change of direction. Gradually speed can be increased and an accent given to the closing of each *battement*.

**Related Exercises**   A *battement soutenu* is performed with a *fondu* on the supporting leg: keeping the gesture leg straight, slide the gesture foot along the floor to *pointe tendue* while bending the supporting leg; return the foot to a closed position while straightening the supporting leg.

A *battement tendu relevé* involves a lowering and relifting of the extended foot: Slide the gesture foot out to *pointe tendue à la seconde*, keeping the weight centered over the supporting foot; release the arches of the foot and lower the heel as the weight centers between both feet; relift the gesture heel and re-arch the foot as the weight returns over the supporting foot; slide the foot into a closed position.

## OTHER BASIC *BATTEMENTS*

### *Battement Dégagé* (baht-MAH*n* day-gah-ZHAY)

**Definition**   A *dégagé* is a *battement* disengaged from the floor; it is sometimes called *battement tendu jeté* ("thrown"), *battement glissé* ("glided"), or simply *dégagé* ("disengaged").

**Purpose**   The chief function of the *dégagé* is to develop speed in pointing the feet. It helps the arches and ankles to become supple and prepares them for the quick movements in jumps. The rapid opening and closing of the leg is the foundation for *allegro* steps with beats (*batterie*). The *dégagé* itself is part of many ballet steps, such as the brushing action in a *glissade*.

**Description**   The movement begins in the same way as *battement tendu*, but the action continues so that the gesture foot leaves the floor a few inches, well pointed, before sliding back to the closed position. The action can be described as a brush of the foot outward and a slide inward.

**Reminders**   The advice for the correct execution of *battements tendus* is equally applicable for *battements dégagés*, except that the toes are allowed to leave the floor. Care must be taken, however, that the toes rise only a very few inches. If the leg is raised too high, the capacity for speed is lost. Faults in many *allegro* steps can be traced to errors made in *dégagés*, especially the failure to

Strong brush from the floor, quick slide to close as inner thighs draw together

touch the pointed toes on the floor before sliding the foot to the closed position. The timing of the exercise should emphasize the closing of the *dégagé*.

**Suggestions**   As in *battements tendus*, the study of *dégagés* begins in first position with the movement done *à la seconde*. It can be broken down as follows: Brush away from the closed position (finishing with the foot slightly off the floor); touch the toes to the floor; slide the foot back to the closed position. Each part of the exercise can receive a separate count, with another count for a hold in the closed position (to allow time for the foot to relax): Brush (count 1), touch the toes (count 2), close (count 3), hold the position (count 4). Later, it can be done in two counts: Brush (count 1), touch the toes (and), close (count 2), hold (and). Eventually the *dégagé* is done with the entire movement happening on the "and," with the closing to position on the count. The breakdown of the exercise can, of course, also be followed in learning *dégagés* to the front and to the back, from third or fifth position, and with a closing to *demi-plié*.

**Related Exercises**   *Battements dégagés en cloche* (ahn KLOHSH) are performed forward and backward through first position and usually occur in a series: Brush the gesture foot forward, slide it back to first position, immediately brush the foot backward, and continue as a swinging, pendulum-like motion through first position.

   *Battements dégagés* may be performed with a *fondu* on the supporting leg in an action similar to *battements soutenus* as previously described.

## *Grand Battement* (grahn baht-MAHn)

**Definition**   The *grand battement* is a large beating action of the leg, a continuation of the basic *battement dégagé*. It sometimes is called *grand battement jeté*.

**Purpose**   The forceful sweeping lift of the leg into the air limbers and stretches the legs (especially at the back of the thighs). It helps to loosen the hip joint, while at the same time strengthening the control of the hip muscles. Properly done, the *grand battement* creates a lightness in the legs necessary for steps of high elevation such as *grand jeté*. It also increases the height of the extension of the legs, valuable for *développés* and other exercises of *adagio*.

**Description**   The movement begins in the same way as the *dégagé* but is continued upward to hip height (higher or lower, depending on the stretch and control of the body); then the leg is lowered with control until the toes touch the floor and the foot closes as in previous exercises for *battements*. *Grands battements* are done to the front, to the side, and to the back.

**Reminders**   Follow all the basic rules of the *battement tendu* and *dégagé*, being especially careful to keep the thighs rotated outward and the weight over the supporting foot. To achieve the desired lightness of the leg, its lift should be initiated by the brush of the foot along the floor, not by the "pickup" of the thigh. The knees must not bend, nor should the heel of the supporting foot leave the floor. Continue to maintain a well-lengthened torso with ribs facing forward, a relaxed neck and throat, stabile but not stiff arms, and the hand held without tension on the *barre*. Note that the pelvis will tip slightly sideward when the leg is raised to hip level *à la seconde*. To permit the leg to rise to the back, the pelvis and torso will tilt slightly forward, and then the body returns to its vertical position as the foot closes.

**Suggestions**   Practice *grands battements* at 45 degrees until proper placement and turnout can be maintained at 90 degrees or higher. Break down the exercise as follows: From a closed position (first, third, or fifth), brush the leg into the air (count 1), lower it to *pointe tendue* (count 2), and return it to the closed

■ Height of the leg for *grand battement à la quatrième devant, à la seconde, à la quatrième derrière* at 90 degrees

Strong, smooth brushes with energy flowing from center of body through hips, legs, and foot

Knees relaxed,
supporting heel released

Hip raised,
thigh turned in

Torso twisted

position (count 3). Eventually the exercise is to be done with the entire movement happening on "and," with the closing of the foot on the count. This must be achieved with control, avoiding any temptation to "drop" the leg as it lowers or to "slam" the foot into the floor!

**Related Exercise**   *Grands battements* may be executed *en cloche* as in *battements dégagés* but with a higher brush of the leg forward and backward, passing smoothly through a turned-out first position each time.

## *Battement Frappé* (baht-MAHn frah-PAY)

**Definition**   A *battement frappé* is a strong brush outward from a raised position at the ankle of the supporting leg; it often is called simply *frappé*, which means "struck."

**Purpose**   The muscles in the foot are stimulated and strengthened by the brush outward along the floor. Articulation of movement through the ankle is improved by the constant alternating motions of extension and release in the foot. This builds speed and flexibility needed in jumping steps, particularly the *jetés*.

**Description**   The *battement frappé à la seconde* begins with the ankle of the gesture foot slightly flexed, the heel touching just above the front of the supporting ankle, and the toes near the floor. The ball of the gesture foot brushes strongly against the floor to *dégagé* position *à la seconde*, knee and foot fully extended. The foot returns quickly to the back of the supporting ankle without touching the floor, ready to begin again.

**Reminders**   The supporting side of the body must remain lifted and lengthened so that the weight remains centered over the supporting foot, thus avoiding either sitting into the hip or pulling away from the supporting heel. The action

■ *Battement frappé à la seconde*

Energetic brush outward from clear placement at supporting ankle

of the *frappé* happens from the knee down, so the thigh does not raise and lower. The ball of the foot should brush briskly along the floor but never pound against the surface. Both the knee and the foot should be taut at the finish of the outward motion.

**Suggestions**   In the early stages, the *frappé* can be done in four counts: Brush to the extended position just off the floor (count 1), hold this position (count 2), return to the position at the supporting leg (count 3), hold (count 4). Later a 3/4 rhythm can be tried: Brush and hold the position (counts 1, 2), return to the supporting leg (count 3). Eventually the *frappé* is done on one count, with the accent on the brush outward and the return on the "and." The exercise can later be done to the front and to the back as well as to the side.

**Related Exercise**   *Battement frappé double* (DOO-bluh) is a doubling of the beating action at the ankle: From a *dégagé* or *pointe tendue* position *à la seconde*, bring the foot inward to beat in front of, and then immediately behind, the supporting ankle, then brush outward as described above. Reverse the action, beating back and then front before brushing outward.

### Petit Battement sur le Cou-de-Pied
(p'TEE baht-MAH*n* suir l'koo-duh-pee-AY)

**Definition**   *Petit battement sur le cou-de-pied* means, literally, "small beat on the neck of the foot."

**Purpose**   The exercise is important in developing speed and precision in movement, particularly for *allegro* steps with beats or rapid accents.

**Description**   The exercise begins with the gesture foot placed *sur le cou-de-pied*, at the ankle of the supporting foot. (The exact position varies in different schools of technique — the foot may be "wrapped" around the ankle, heel in front and toes in back; it may be extended downward along the side of the ankle; it may be fully pointed in front or in back of the ankle; or it may be

Small, rapid gestures with a bright playful quality

relaxed, heel touching the ankle and all five toes on the floor in *demi-pointe* position.) The *battements* consist of small, rapid out-and-in movements of the gesture foot as it rebounds slightly from each contact in front of and behind the supporting ankle.

**Reminders**   Keep the heel of the beating foot well forward and do not change the shape of the foot as it moves out and in around the supporting ankle. Keep the thigh of the gesture leg pressed well outward, hip remaining in place, and the knee relaxed so that the action of the beat is made with the lower leg only.

**Suggestions**   To sense the quality of moving the lower leg freely from the knee joint: Stand sideways to the *barre* with the legs in parallel position, flex the outside leg so that the ball of the foot rests lightly on the floor, and place the free hand on the raised thigh. Keep the thigh immobile and the knee relaxed as the lower leg swings evenly forward and back. Next, perform this exercise with a turnout, allowing the working foot to swing evenly across in front and in back of the supporting foot. Later, speed is increased and accents can be added (back, *front*, hold; back, *front*, hold; and so on).

## CIRCULAR MOVEMENTS

Circular movements of the leg, either along the ground or in the air, are important elements of *barre* work, later incorporated into exercises in center floor as well.

### Rond de Jambe à Terre (rohn duh zhahnb ah TAIR)

**Definition**   There are over a dozen exercises bearing the general term *rond de jambe* (literally, "circle or round of the leg"). The most basic is *rond de jambe à terre* (or *par terre*), the gesture foot describing a semicircle on the ground. When the foot travels in an arc from the front to the back, it is called an "outward"

■ *Rond de jambe à terre en dehors*

*Pointes tendues* positions joined by a smooth arcing motion, passing through first position to continue

(*en dehors*) *rond de jambe*. When it travels from the back to the front, it is called an "inward" (*en dedans*) *rond de jambe*.

**Purpose**   In *ronds de jambe*, the muscles and ligaments of the hip are exercised to allow the leg to move freely in a circular motion without disturbing the immobility of the torso. Characteristics of this movement are found in such steps as *pas de basque*.

**Description**   For *ronds de jambe en dehors*, extend the gesture foot forward from first position in the same way as for *battement tendu devant*, carry the toes in an arc along the ground through *pointe tendue à la seconde* to *pointe tendue derrière* behind first position. Then slide the foot forward to first position in the same way as the closing of a *battement tendu*. The direction of the entire exercise is reversed for *ronds de jambe en dedans*. The exercise usually is done to a 3/4 rhythm, with an entire semicircle completed during one measure. A series of *ronds de jambe* may be executed continuously without pause or with accents given at *pointe tendue positions devant* or *derrière*.

**Reminders**   The toes of the gesture foot remain in contact with the floor during the entire exercise. The gesture foot must remain fully arched as it traces the arc of the semicircle, taking care not to shorten the arc near the *pointes tendues* positions to the front or to the back. As the foot passes through first position, it should relax but take care not to roll. Both legs must remain thoroughly extended throughout the exercise with the body lengthened upward and centered over the supporting foot. The supporting leg must resist any temptation to rotate inward, thus defeating one purpose of *rond de jambe*: improvement of turnout.

**Suggestions**   The *rond de jambe* is best learned slowly, with a pause in each position of the arc (front, side, back) and at the first position.

**Related Exercises**   A helpful exercise for emphasizing turnout is the *demi-rond de jambe à terre*: To perform *en dehors* from first position, extend the foot

Coordination of opposites: strong verticality of support side of body with horizontal
circling of gesture leg

to *pointe tendue devant* and quickly carry it *à la seconde*, hold at the *pointe
tendue* position, then close to first position. Reverse the action for *demi-rond de
jambe en dedans*.

A *demi-rond de jambe* lifted to 45 degrees in the air — that is, at half height
or *à la demi-hauteur* (ah la d'mee-oh-TUHR) — introduces the important pelvic,
torso, and weight adjustments necessary when the leg travels in the air from
one direction to another: To perform *en dehors*, brush the gesture foot forward
from first or fifth position as in a *battement dégagé* to 45 degrees *à la quatrième
devant*; leading with the foot, carry the leg *à la seconde* at the same height,
maintaining turnout and keeping the weight centered over the supporting foot;

lower to *pointe tendue* and close to first or fifth position. To continue *en dehors*: Brush the gesture foot *à la seconde* to 45 degrees; as the foot leads around at the same level to *quatrième derrière*, the pelvis will tilt slightly forward so the torso must lengthen upward and also forward, allowing the center of weight to shift more forward; lower to *pointe tendue*, returning the body to its normal upright position as the foot closes to first or fifth position. Reverse the actions to perform the exercise *en dedans*.

## ADDITIONAL BASIC EXERCISES

Out of the multitude of possible exercises to be included in *barre* work, only four more are given here. Again, the reader is reminded that no "proper" order of exercises has been implied in this chapter. Rather, exercises have been grouped according to general characteristics, with the following exercises sharing a folding-and-unfolding design for the leg or for the torso.

### *Battement Retiré* (baht-MAH*n* ruh-tih-RAY)

**Definition**    The *battement retiré* is a "withdrawing" of the gesture foot from the floor until it touches the front, side, or back of the supporting knee. The term *passé* is sometimes used when the foot passes from fifth position front to fifth position back and vice versa.

**Purpose**    This exercise is an integral part of many movements in ballet, such as *développés* and *pas de chats*. It has great value in warming up the thighs and in strengthening the muscles in the waist and back. *Retirés* (or *passés*) also can improve balance and turnout.

**Description**    From fifth position, crisply draw up the front leg, keeping the toes in contact with the supporting leg, to a fully pointed position in front or to the hollow of the supporting knee; return the foot to the closed position as the weight centers again over both feet. When the back foot performs a *retiré*, the

■ *Retiré*                                                      ■ **Incorrect** *retiré*

Stabile balance over support and clear design of gesture leg

toes of the gesture foot draw up either behind or to the hollow of the supporting knee.

**Reminders**   The thighs of both legs must remain well turned out and the pelvis level throughout the exercise. The heel of the gesture foot does not touch the supporting leg in the *retiré* positions. Initiate the action of *retiré* by the push of the foot from the floor rather than by a pickup of the thigh; keep the elongation of the pointed foot as long as possible during the return, releasing first the toes, then the ball of the foot, and finally the heel into the closed position.

**Suggestions**   To ensure correct body alignment, learn the exercise facing the *barre*. Use third position if fifth is not yet secure and a lower *retiré* position if the pelvis cannot remain level when the thigh is raised. Practice slowly in sequential action: Sharply arch the foot just in front of and above the supporting ankle as the body centers over the supporting leg, draw the foot up to *retiré* position, hold, and return to the beginning position.

**Related Exercises**   When executed from a *demi-plié* to a *relevé* in the *retiré* position, the exercise becomes an important practice for *pirouettes*. Another exercise is preliminary to *rond de jambe en l'air*: *Dégagé à la seconde* to 45 degrees, bring the toes to *retiré* position without lowering the thigh, extend the leg again at the same height, continue in a series, and then lower to a closed position.

## Développé (day-vloh-PAY)

**Definition**   In the *développé*, the gesture leg is "developed" (unfolded) from the floor to an open position at 45 degrees or higher to the front, side, or back.

**Purpose**   This is one of the most fundamental exercises of *adagio* (the slow, sustained movements of ballet), for it is the method by which the leg can arrive at many ballet positions, such as *arabesque*. *Développés*, done repeatedly as an

■ *Développé à la seconde*

Extending a design into space

exercise, have great strengthening value for the muscles of the abdomen, legs, and back, thus improving the ability to sustain an extension of the leg in the air.

**Description**   The gesture foot is drawn up along the supporting leg to a *retiré* position, then smoothly unfolded to the appropriate height *à la quatrième devant*, *à la seconde*, or *à la quatrième derrière*.

**Reminders**   The gesture foot arches as soon as it leaves the closed position, and it must travel close to the supporting leg until it reaches the *retiré* position. Establish the appropriate height of the thigh, and then unfold the lower leg at that level. Maintain a strong turnout of both legs, torso lengthened upward with the ribs facing forward and the body centered over the supporting foot. Note that the pelvis will tilt slightly sideward in a *développé* to 90 degrees *à la seconde*, and it will tilt slightly forward in *développés* to the back. Briefly hold the extended position before lowering the leg smoothly to the closed position, the weight centering over both feet.

**Suggestions**   First master the control and balance necessary for the *retiré* before attempting the *développé*. Ideally, the *développé* should be done slowly and smoothly in one continuous flow from the closed position to the extended position. Nevertheless, it is helpful to practice the exercise with slight pauses of the foot, first at the ankle, then at the knee, then at the halfway position before full extension, and finally at the full height of the *développé*. It is best first to learn the leg movements alone before adding coordinated arm movements.

### *Battement Fondu* (baht-MAH*n* foh*n*-DIU)

**Definition**   *Battement fondu* ("melting") is a compound exercise consisting of a bending of the supporting leg and then a straightening of that leg as the gesture leg unfolds from a *cou-de-pied* position to *pointe tendue*.

**Description**   From *pointe tendue à la seconde*, bring the fully arched foot to *cou-de-pied devant* as the supporting leg bends. (A bend on one leg is a *fondu*.) Simultaneously straighten both legs as the gesture foot opens to *pointe tendue devant*. Continue with the same action, unfolding the leg *à la seconde* and then *à la quatrième derrière*.

**Reminders**   Emphasize equal turnout and harmonious bending and straightening of both legs. The gesture foot remains fully arched throughout the exercise.

**Suggestions**   A clear understanding of the positions of *cou-de-pied devant* and *derrière* should precede study of this exercise. To counteract any tendency to sink or drop into the *fondu*, it is helpful to lift the foot slightly off the floor from *pointe tendue*, as though the leg takes a breath before the knees bend.

**Related Exercises**   *Battement fondu* may be done *en l'air*, unfolding the leg to *dégagé* height or higher, depending on development of the necessary strength and control of the legs, pelvis, and torso. Later a *relevé* may accompany the unfolding of the leg *en l'air*.

Smooth harmony of legs unfolding simultaneously

## *Port de Bras au Corps Cambré* (por duh BRAH oh kor kahn-BRAY)

**Definition**   *Port de bras au corps cambré* means, literally, "carriage of the arms with an arched body." Usually the term is used to describe the bending of the body backward or sideward from the waist. The forward bend from the hips is sometimes termed *penché* or *port de corps* forward.

**Purpose**   This exercise is important because it involves movements of the head, arms, and torso, and not, as in all other *barre* exercises, movement of the legs. It also limbers and relaxes the upper body and coordinates arm and head movements — all necessary for fluidity of motion.

**Description**   In the forward bend, the torso lengthens upward as it begins to reach forward from the hip joints, the spine remaining extended as long as

■ *Port de corps* forward

■ *Cambré* backward

■ *Cambré* sideward

Coordinated movement flow into the space around the body

■ **Incorrect positions**

Weight pushed back,
spine swayed

Knees bent,
pelvis released

Torso twisted,
weight off center

possible; then it curves downward until the head is near the knees. Return to the upright position is made by retracing the path of the forward bend or by uncurling (rolling up) through the spine.

The *cambré* backward begins with a lift in the chest and face, usually as the outside arm rises toward the ceiling; then the upper back arches while the lower back and pelvis remain upright. Ribs remain facing forward, but the head may turn in the direction of the raised arm. Return to the upright position is made by retracing the path of the backward bend or by opening the arm outward to second position as the back straightens.

The *cambré* sideward occurs from the waist with the torso well lengthened. One arm, raised over the head, reaches sideward in the direction of the bend, and the head may either turn to that direction or remain focused front. Return to the upright position is made by retracing the path of the sideward bend or by bringing the arm forward of the body and then to the side as the torso straightens.

**Reminders**   The legs remain straight and vertical with the weight of the body evenly distributed on both feet when these exercises are done from any of the five positions of the feet. Avoid straining the neck, raising the shoulders, or shortening the lower spine, especially in the *cambré* backward. All movements should be done smoothly, with the arm flowing into gently curved positions.

**Suggestions**   These bending exercises should be learned in first position before they are attempted in other positions. Learn the forward bend as a half-bend; that is, stretch forward until the upper body is parallel to the floor (or as parallel as possible, given the stretch in the legs) and then return to the upright position. The bend backward at first can be learned facing the *barre*. An intake of breath just before and during the bend is helpful.

## STRETCHES

Stretches are matters of some controversy among ballet teachers. There are those who advocate stretches and incorporate them into the classwork. Others feel that *barre* exercises alone give proper limbering and that most other stretching exercises are artificial and useless ("If you are limber, stretches are unnecessary; if you aren't limber, stretches won't help!"). All would agree, however, that stretches should be attempted only when the body is thoroughly warmed up—after the completion of *barre* work or at the end of class.

It is the author's opinion that certain stretches, if done correctly, are useful to certain bodies, but, for ballet, flexibility must be attained *along with* strength and endurance. Therefore, a few words of general advice are offered rather than an outline of specific limbering exercises.

**Suggestions**   Allow the body to relax into the stretch. Forceful bouncing or reaching, which causes one set of muscles to tighten as another set is stretched, defeats limbering. All stretches should be done slowly and smoothly. The correct position of the foot on the floor, the lift of the arch, and the alignment of foot with leg must not be sacrificed during stretches in a standing position. Do your own stretching. Relying on others to lift, to bend, or to push your limbs and torso can be dangerous. And, finally, do stretches only when the body is fully warmed up.

# CHAPTER 3

# BALLET TECHNIQUE: CENTER WORK

When *barre* work is completed, the mechanics of ballet technique are brought into the center floor. To the movements of the legs and feet now are added movements of the head, carriages of the arms (*ports de bras*), and positions of the shoulders (*épaulements*), which bring artistic life to even the simplest ballet exercise. Using all these elements — the entire body — to create harmonious designs in space is the challenge of center work.

## DIRECTIONS OF THE STUDIO/STAGE

Ballet is taught as a performing art, even though 99 percent of all ballet students may never set foot on a professional stage. Positions and movements of center floor work are based on the assumption that an audience is at the front of the room. At all times, the dancer/student must be aware of body line in relation to the eye of that audience. The parts of the stage have directional names that also are useful in the studio: *Downstage* is toward the audience. *Upstage* is away from the audience. *Stage right* is to the dancer's right as the dancer faces the audience. *Stage left* is then to the dancer's left. These directional names remain constant, no matter which way the dancer faces.

Much of beginning work is done facing the "audience" (a direction known as *de face*, although movement made toward the audience often is said to be done *en face*). When asked to face a corner direction, students should first imagine themselves standing in the center of a "private" stage about a yard square, then face the corner of that square, rather than the actual corner of the studio, and,

Audience
Downstage

Downstage left          Downstage right

Upstage left          Upstage right

Upstage

from the neck downward, align the body with the downstage corner of that imaginary stage square. For practicing movements of the arms and positions of the body, a thirty-six-inch square, complete with diagonals (as in the diagram above), can be outlined on the floor with masking tape. Do not, however, imagine solid walls around the small square, for the poses must never appear tight or static. Even the stillness of the body must look alive, as though the limbs might grow beyond the confines of the studio walls or ceiling.

## PORT DE BRAS (por duh BRAH)

Center floor work often begins with *port de bras* ("carriage of the arms"), which refers not only to arm movements but also to groups of exercises for the arms. The earlier term *corps et bras* ("body and arms") is in some ways more descriptive because the head, shoulders, and torso are very much involved, with energy for the arm movements coming from the dancer's back.

An infinite variety of *port de bras* is possible within the framework provided by the positions of the arms. There are, however, two fundamental exercises of *port de bras* that are the most essential and the most frequently used. They illustrate ballet's basic rule for arm movements: When the arms move from a low to a high position, they travel in front of the body through the position *en avant* (*bras avant*) and then outward through second position as they lower. These movements look deceptively simple, but, in the words of Agrippina Vaganova, "*Port de bras* is the most difficult part of the dance, requiring the greatest amount of work and concentration."[1]

Again, variations of style exist, but the following descriptions outline the two basic exercises:

■ Exercise 1

### Exercise 1

1. The starting pose: Face downstage left in third or fifth position (right foot front), the arms *en bas*, the head inclined to the left and slightly lowered.
2. Raise the arms *en avant* and, at the same time, lean the torso slightly forward from the waist.
3. Open the palms slightly and carry both arms to second position while the head turns and inclines to the right. During this movement, the torso can also lean to the right a small degree, and the eyes follow in the direction of the right hand. The hips and shoulders do not twist but remain in alignment facing the original downstage corner.
4. Lower the arms to the starting pose as the head simultaneously returns to its original position.

### Exercise 2

1. The starting pose: same as in Exercise 1.
2. Raise the arms *en avant* as the torso inclines slightly forward and the head remains inclined to the left.
3. Continue to raise the arms *en haut* while the torso straightens and the head lifts and then inclines to the right.

4. Open both arms to second position as the torso leans slightly to the right and the eyes follow in the direction of the right hand. The hips and shoulders do not twist.

5. Lower the arms to the starting pose as the head simultaneously returns to its original position.

■ Exercise 2

Each *port de bras* is done several times in succession, and each sequence is practiced to the other side as well. Traditionally, most center exercises that are done diagonally begin toward the downstage left corner and then are repeated to the right corner. Exercises are done slowly and smoothly so that the movement flows through, but does not stop, in any one position. Take care that the hands stay centered on the body as they travel from the *bras bas* position to *bras hauts*, that the shoulders do not rise or twist, and that the fingers do not spread open.

This brief discussion of *port de bras* ends with a further observation from Vaganova:

> Only the ability to find the proper position for her arms lends a finesse to the artistic expression of the dancer, and renders full harmony to her dance. The head gives it the finishing touch, adds beauty to the entire design. The look, the glance, the eyes, crown it all.[2]

## CENTER EXERCISES AND *ÉPAULEMENT* (ay-pohl-MAH*n*)

Center work includes a repetition of numerous *barre* exercises without the aid of the *barre*. Because these *exercises au milieu* (eg-zehr-SEESS oh mee-LYUH) are often done on alternate feet, they can help develop greater balance, coordination, and control.

An example is a series of *battements tendus* traveling forward: From fifth position right foot back, *battement tendu à la seconde* with the right foot, close front in fifth position; repeat with the left foot. Continue in this way, alternating right and left legs eight or sixteen times.

The exercise is then reversed so that the *battements tendus* close in fifth position back. Beginning students generally practice these and similar exercises *de face* — that is, directly toward the front of the room. Later an important embellishment is added, enlivening an otherwise flat appearance. It is called *épaulement*. Although this literally means "shouldering," it encompasses movement of the head and upper body as well as the shoulders. The traditional rule for *épaulement* is: In steps that travel forward, the head and shoulders are aligned with the foot that closes front, the head turning slightly toward the gesture foot. In steps that travel backward, the head and shoulders are in opposition to the foot that closes back, the head inclining slightly away from the gesture foot.

Therefore, the exercise of *battements tendus* traveling forward using *épaulement* is: From fifth position right foot in back, extend the right foot *à la seconde* and, simultaneously, bring the right shoulder slightly forward of the left, with the head slightly turned to the right. The head and right shoulder are now aligned with the right or gesture foot. Close to fifth position front without changing the *épaulement*. The exercise is repeated with the left leg, so that the left shoulder is brought forward, and the head is turned to the left.

The exercise of *battements tendus* traveling backward with *épaulement* is: From fifth position left foot in front, extend the left foot *à la seconde* and, simultaneously, bring the right shoulder slightly forward of the left, with the head slightly inclined to the right. The head and right shoulder are now in opposition to the left or gesture foot. Close to fifth position behind without changing the *épaulement*. The exercise continues alternating legs, the shoulders and head always in opposition to the gesture leg.

The degree and style of *épaulement* used is a matter of preference, but a general rule is to keep the hips facing directly front rather than turning or twisting. Focus of the eyes may remain forward or move slightly toward the diagonal indicated by the forward shoulder.

*Épaulement* is not confined to center exercises. The principles of alignment and opposition are used constantly in *adagio* phrases, which are done later in the center. The final stage of instruction, the *allegro*, includes many steps that are improved greatly by the addition of a little shouldering action. However, the student needs a solid understanding of the mechanics of these steps before embellishing them with *épaulement*.

■ **Traveling forward**

■ **Traveling backward**

## POSITIONS OF THE BODY

The classic line of ballet is built on the alignment of the body in space, as well as on alignment within the body. There are eleven positions of the body in space, from which infinite variations of poses are possible. They are learned first with the extended leg at *pointe tendue*; later, with the leg raised to 45 degrees, and then to 90 degrees.

### Facing Front

Beginning students quite soon are familiar with the three positions of the body that face directly front (*en face*), or toward the audience:

*À la quatrième devant* (ah la ka-tree-EHM duh-VAHn): The extended leg is in fourth position front; the arms are in second position; the head, hips, and shoulders face directly front.

*À la quatrième derrière* (deh-reeAIR): The extended leg is in fourth position back; the arms are in second position; the head, hips, and shoulders face directly front.

*À la seconde* (ah la suh-GOHnD): The extended leg is in second position; the arms are in second position; the head, hips, and shoulders face directly front.

### On the Diagonal

Once the front-facing positions are mastered, the student is introduced to poses on the diagonal. The terms for these poses, translated literally, are: *croisé* ("crossed"), *effacé* ("shaded"), *écarté* ("separated" or "thrown wide apart"), and *épaulé* ("shouldered"). Each can be done to the front (*devant*) and to the back (*derrière*). Stylistic preferences determine the height and degree of curve of the arms and the incline of the head and torso. The following description represents a stylistic choice for these diagonal positions.

*Croisé* (krawh-ZAY) *devant:* The dancer faces either downstage corner; the leg nearer the audience extends to fourth position front; the arm opposite that extended leg is *en haut*, and the other arm is *demi-seconde*; the torso and head incline slightly toward the low arm.

*Croisé derrière:* The dancer faces either downstage corner; the leg farther from the audience extends to fourth position back; the arm opposite the extended leg is *en haut*, and the other arm is *demi-seconde*; the head and torso incline very slightly toward the low arm so that the dancer appears to be looking at the audience from under the high arm.

*Effacé* (eh-fah-SAY) *devant:* The dancer faces either downstage corner; the leg farther from the audience extends to fourth position front; the arm opposite the extended leg is *en haut*, and the other arm is *demi-seconde*; the body leans very slightly back from the waist, and the head inclines toward the high arm.

*Effacé derrière:* The dancer faces either downstage corner; the leg nearer the audience extends to fourth position back; the arm on the same side as the extended leg is *en haut*, and the other arm is *demi-seconde*; the body leans slightly forward over the supporting foot; the head turns and rises slightly toward the hand that is high.

*Écarté* (ay-kar-TAY) *devant:* The dancer faces either downstage corner; the leg nearer the audience extends to second position; the arm on the same side as the extended leg is *en haut*, and the other arm is *demi-seconde*; the torso is erect; the head turns and rises slightly toward the hand that is high.

*Écarté derrière:* The dancer faces either downstage corner; the leg farther from the audience extends to second position; the arm on the same side as the extended leg is *en haut*, and the other arm is *demi-seconde*; the torso and head incline slightly toward the hand that is low.

*Épaulé* (ah-poh-LAY) *devant:* The dancer faces either downstage corner; the leg nearer the audience extends to fourth position back; the arm nearer the audience extends forward, and the other arm extends backward; the torso turns slightly from the waist so that the back arm is slightly visible to the audience; the head inclines toward the front shoulder.

*Épaulé derrière:* This position is exactly the same as *épaulé devant*, except that the dancer faces either of the upstage corners.

Positions of the body can be practiced in sequential action as a center floor exercise. The following sequence represents that of the Cecchetti method. The eight positions are illustrated here as though seen from the back so that the reader may relate to the poses more easily.

■ *Croisé devant*　　■ *Quatrième devant*　　■ *Écarté devant*　　■ *Effacé devant*

■ *À la seconde*

■ *Épaulé devant*

■ *Quatrième derrière*

■ *Croisé derrière*

## OTHER POSES OF THE BODY

*Attitude* and *arabesque* are two poses most frequently associated with ballet. As the reader readily can imagine by now, variations of these poses are practically unlimited, and differences of style do exist. Still, certain fundamental rules remain constant.

### *Attitude* (ah-tee-TEWD)

The ballet *attitude* is a pose on one leg, the other leg lifted, well turned out and bent at the knee with the lower leg and foot opened away from the body. Carlo Blasis, an early nineteenth-century ballet master and author of important dance

■ *Attitude croisée derrière*

■ *Attitude croisée devant*

■ *Attitude à terre*

54

technique manuals, considered the *attitude* to be the most elegant but the most difficult pose in dancing. He believed it to be a kind of imitation of the statue of Mercury, messenger of the gods, by the artist Giovanni da Bologna.[3] However, in today's technique, unlike in the Renaissance statue, the thigh and knee are lifted, well turned out, and level with, or higher than, the raised foot.

Mercury

When the leg is lifted to the back, the pose is known as *attitude derrière*. Another variation calls for the leg to be lifted to the front, well turned out, the knee bent, and the foot raised as high as possible. This pose is known as *attitude devant*. These two *attitudes* most commonly occur in the *croisé* or *effacé* direction with one arm raised *en haut* and the other opened *à la seconde*, usually referred to as "*attitude* position" of the arms.

**Reminders**   *Attitudes* require a well-turned-out supporting leg that maintains a strong verticality into the hip socket so that the body weight is balanced over the supporting foot. The abdominal muscles and spine lengthen upward so that the torso and pelvis do not lean to the side.

**Related Poses**   *Attitude à deux bras* — that is with both arms *en haut* (or *en avant*) — is an attractive alternative, especially helpful in stabilizing the *attitude* position. *Attitude à terre* is a pose frequently used to begin or end a movement phrase: Standing *en face* or *croisé*, bend the upstage leg, foot pointed on the ground either directly behind the supporting ankle or crossed behind the opposite shoulder with knees close together, and arms in *attitude* position or some other pleasing shape.

## *Arabesque* (ah-ra-BESK)

Perhaps the "ultimate" pose in today's ballet is the *arabesque*, in which the body is balanced over one foot with the other leg fully extended behind. The arms also are extended, palms down, creating a long, symmetrical line from fingertips to toetips. Blasis surmised that the design and name were derived from ancient paintings, which in turn had been influenced by the Moorish and Arabic taste for architectural ornaments and embellishments.[4]

*Arabesques* are learned *à terre* — that is, the toes of the extended leg touching the ground. Later, as the leg is gradually raised *en l'air*, the pelvis responds by tilting forward in adjustment, allowing the lower spine (lumbar vertebrae) to remain extended. At the same time, the torso lengthens upward and slightly forward through the upper spine (thoracic vertebrae) and head as the body weight centers over the ball of the supporting foot.

The arms are extended, rather than curved, with the fingers also extended and the palms facing the floor. Usually, the height of the arms balances the height of the leg, enabling an unbroken line to be drawn from the fingers of the front hand to the toes of the extended foot. Thus, the lower the leg, the higher the front arm, and, as the leg rises, the front arm moves into a more horizontal line.

**Reminders**   As the leg lifts to the back, it must be well turned out from the hip, which causes a slight rotation in the lower spine. At the same time, the supporting leg counters this pull by maintaining its outward rotation. Strong abdominal control through the waist is required to maintain the balance of this position.

Four basic *arabesques* are given here. The extended leg is pictured at different levels, *à terre* to 90 degrees, any of which may be done in any of the *arabesques*.

First *arabesque*: The dancer stands in profile to the audience; the leg nearer the audience extends to the back; the forward arm corresponds to the supporting leg; the other arm is taken slightly back of second position but without strain to the shoulder; the eyes focus over the forward hand.

Second *arabesque*: The dancer stands as in first *arabesque*, except the arms are reversed so that the forward arm is in opposition to the supporting leg; the head may incline toward the audience.

Third *arabesque* Cecchetti method (or *arabesque à deux bras*): The dancer
stands as in first *arabesque*, but with both arms extended forward; the
arm farther from the audience is slightly higher; the focus is between the
two hands.

Third *arabesque* Russian school: The dancer faces the downstage corner with
the upstage leg raised in *arabesque*; the forward arm is in opposition to
the supporting leg; ribs, shoulders, and head focus toward the downstage
corner.

**Related Poses** All the *arabesques* described can be done with a bend of the
supporting leg. This pose, known as *arabesque en fondue*, frequently precedes
or makes a transition to another movement. A common pose in later stages of
training is *arabesque penchée* (pahn-SHAY), in which the leg is raised very high,
causing the pelvis and torso to tilt well forward while still maintaining the

■ First *arabesque en fondue*

lifted shape of the spine in *arabesque*. The head and forward arm are low, counterbalancing the raised foot, which is the highest point of the pose.

## CONNECTING MOVEMENTS

Connecting movements are those which link various poses, prepare for certain actions, and/or move the dancer from one location to another. Although transitional in purpose, these steps enhance the flow of movement, helping to keep it vibrant rather than static. They are connecting movements in quite another sense as well: They developed from steps used in social and theatrical court dances in the seventeenth century, thus linking today's ballet to its aristocratic origins.

### *Glissé* (glee-SAY)

**Definition**   Meaning to glide, this movement has a sliding quality that relates it to *chassé* (see Chapter 4), a term by which it also is known.

**Description**   *Glissé* may be done forward, backward or sideward, *en face* as well as on the diagonal. To perform forward or *en avant*: From a *demi-plié* in fifth position, slide the front foot forward to fourth position *demi-plié*, keeping the pelvis level and legs evenly turned out; smoothly transfer the weight completely to the front leg, straightening the knees and extending the back foot to *pointe tendue derrière*.

**Suggestions**   Begin to transfer the weight to the front leg from the fourth position *demi-plié* before allowing the back heel to raise. Sense the spine pushing to the front as the transition is made onto the forward leg. Smoothly coordinate the movements of the arms with the legs, usually moving the arms through *en avant* during the glide into fourth position and then opening the arms to a desired position as the legs straighten.

## *Tombé* (tohn-BAY)

**Definition**   Meaning falling or fallen, *tombé* is any movement in which the dancer, having extended the gesture leg, falls forward, sideward, or backward into a *fondu* on that gesture leg.

**Description**   To perform *tombé en avant*: From fifth position *demi-pointes*, *dégagé* the front leg forward as the arms rise to a desired position; fall well forward into a lunge on the gesture leg, usually moving the arms to another desired position. The back leg remains extended with the foot at *pointe tendue* or raised in the air.

■ *Tombé en avant*

■ *A tombé à la seconde*

**Suggestions**   The falling action is a soft, controlled one with contact to the floor being made smoothly through the entire foot (toe-ball-heel) into a *fondu*. The body weight remains lifted upward out of the hips and through the waist as it centers immediately over the well-turned-out *fondu* leg.

### *Piqué* (pee-KAY)

**Definition**   A sharp step in any direction taken directly onto the *demi-pointe* of a straight gesture leg. The brisk action reflects the literal meaning of the term—pricked. Also called *posé* (poh-ZAY).

**Description**   To perform *en avant*: Facing downstage right with the right foot front in fifth position, *dégagé* the right foot forward to *effacé* as the supporting leg lowers into *fondu*; push strongly from the supporting foot and step well

■ *Piqué sur le cou-de-pied*

forward with a slight springing action onto the right *demi-pointe*, quickly lifting the left leg to a desired position; close the left foot to fifth position back.

**Suggestions**    Initial practice can be a step onto the whole foot before attempting a step onto *demi-pointe*. Emphasis should be on taking the center of the body well forward onto the straight supporting leg. Some usual positions for the raised leg in a *piqué en avant* include *sur le cou-de-pied derrière*, *retiré derrière*, and *arabesque*. It is wise to learn them in that order. Instead of the finish to fifth position, the raised leg can lower in *fondu* directly beneath the forward leg, which then once more extends in *dégagé* to continue a series of *piqués*. Or, from a *piqué* in *arabesque*, the raised leg can move forward into a *tombé*.

### Pas de Bourrée (pah duh boo-RAY)

**Definition**    The *bourrée* was a French folk dance form, court dance form, and musical form. The *pas de bourrée*, or "*bourrée* step," had dozens of variations in early eighteenth-century dance technique. Today's ballet vocabulary contains considerably fewer, with six versions commonly appearing in elementary classes. Although the actual performance of the steps has changed, now, as then, the *pas de bourrée* involves three movements — either three shifts of weight or two shifts of weight and then a closing to position.

**Description**    In general, if the preparation is a *dégagé*, the *pas de bourrée* will finish in fifth position *demi-plié*. If, however, the *pas de bourrée* begins with one foot raised in front or back of the ankle, it usually will finish in a *fondu* with the other foot in the raised position. The first method is described and illustrated here.

   *Pas de bourrée dessous:* From fifth position, left foot front or back, *demi-plié* and *dégagé à la seconde* with the left foot (this is a preparatory movement that occurs on count "and"). Draw the left foot to fifth position in back of the right foot as both feet rise to the *demi-pointes*. Immediately open the right foot to a small second position and step onto *demi-pointe*. Close the left foot front in fifth position *demi-plié*.

*Pas de bourrée dessus:* Perform as above, but after the preparatory *dégagé*, step in *front*, then to the side, and close the first foot in back.

*Pas de bourrée derrière:* Perform as above, but step in back, then to the side, and close in back.

*Pas de bourrée devant:* Perform as above, but step in front, then to the side, and close in front.

*Pas de bourrée en arrière:* From *pointe tendue* in fourth position, right foot front, bring the right foot to fifth position front stepping onto *demi-pointe*, immediately open the left foot, and take a small step backward onto *demi-pointe*; close the right foot front in *fondu* as the left foot extends to *pointe tendue* in fourth position back.

*Pas de bourrée en avant:* Perform as above, but begin from fourth position back, bring the foot to fifth position, step forward, and close back as the other foot extends to the front.

Both the *pas de bourrée en arrière* and *en avant* may start from fifth position with a preparatory *dégagé* to the *tendue* position, and they may finish in fifth position *demi-plié*. They are usually performed to the *effacé* or *croisé* directions.
**Other Forms** *Pas de bourrée piqué* means that the feet are picked up sharply to the height of the ankle or knee on each step. In *pas de bourrée fondu*, the second step is made in *fondu* rather than to *demi-pointe*. In more advanced training, *pas de bourrée* is done *en tournant*, either *en dehors* (turning outward with a *pas de bourrée dessous*) or *en dedans* (turning inward with a *pas de*

*bourrée dessus*). Tiny running steps traveling in any direction are called *pas de bourrée couru*. They are done with the feet tightly crossed in fifth position on the *demi-pointes* (later on full point for advanced women students) or without turnout (in parallel position).

### Pas Marché (pah mahr-SHAY)

**Definition**   A walking step executed in an elegant, dignified manner.

**Description**   Steps are taken with the feet only slightly turned out. The weight is transferred smoothly through the foot, toes contacting the floor first. Each step can be preceded either by a very small *développé* or a low *dégagé* with the foot well extended. The heels scarcely touch the floor, the desired image being one of nonaffected assurance but decidedly not pedestrian casualness.

## TURNS

Most poses and steps can be done *en tournant*, or turning. They at once become more exciting to watch and more challenging to perform. Probably no aspect of ballet has received more analysis by teachers (or attention by students) than the *pirouette*, a complete spin on one foot.

Any turn demands a correctly aligned body whose feet, legs, and back have been strengthened by elementary ballet exercises. To this strong vertical balance is added the first principle of turning—the clear focus of the eyes on a fixed point and the quick snap of the head, called *spotting*.

## SPOTTING

For a turn in place, the gaze stays momentarily on a fixed point straight in front of the body as the turn begins. The head then leads the turn, arriving back at the fixed focal point before the rest of the body. This manipulation of the head and focus of the eyes allow the dancer to turn without becoming dizzy, and they contribute to the momentum for fast turns. The origin of the trick of spotting is not known. Erik Bruhn, a fine dancer who turns quite naturally, suggests that it perhaps was "originally an accidental discovery which some dancer later embodied in his teaching and which eventually became a universally accepted practice."[5]

Practice

Students who find turning less than second nature (and there are many who do) can become acquainted with spotting by revolving slowly in place while taking small steps on both feet. The focus remains on a fixed point to the front as the turn begins, and then the head snaps around to finish the revolution before the rest of the body. The head is erect, and the fixed focal point is on a line level with the eyes.

■ Spotting for turns

## TURNS ON TWO FEET

Once the principle of spotting is understood, the student practices turns on two feet. These are done in place as *soutenus en tournant*, or traveling as *tours de basque* and *tours chaînés*.

### Soutenu en Tournant (soo-teh-NEW ah*n* toor-NAN*n*)

**Definition**   Meaning "sustained turning," this movement most commonly is executed *en dedans*, or inwards.

**Description**   From fifth position, left foot back, slide the left foot to the side while bending the right knee (or *tombé* onto the right leg). Draw the left foot to fifth position front—either by closing straight in or by making a *demi-rond de jambe en dedans*—while simultaneously rising to the *demi-pointes* and turning right, thus facing the back of the room. (The left foot will be in front of the right.) Continue turning to the right on both feet until facing the front of the

■ *Soutenu en tournant en dedans*

room once more, leaving the left foot in back in fifth position. The turn also is called *assemblé soutenu en tournant en dedans*, which implies a slight spring to the *demi-pointe* position. Reverse the movements to perform the turn *en dehors*.

**Suggestions**   The leg that opens and closes must stay straight. Open the arms to second position as the foot goes to the side; close the arms *en avant*, or raise them *en haut* by going through *en avant* position, as the turn is made.

Preparatory Exercises

The mechanics of these turns can be practiced at the *barre* as simple *battements soutenus*: Slide one foot *à la seconde* while the supporting leg bends; close in fifth position either *à terre* (heels on the ground) or *en relevé*. Later, half-turns can be practiced at the *barre* and in center, and, finally, the complete turn can be done in center.

### *Tour de Basque* (toor duh BAHSK)

**Definition**   *Tour de basque* (literally, "Basque turn") is also known as *petit pas de basque sur les pointes* ("little Basque step on the points"), reflecting a kinship with steps traditional to dances of the Basque people. (See Chapter 4, "*Pas de Basque*.")

**Description**   From fifth position, right foot front, brush the right foot slightly off the ground to the front and then open it out to the side (*demi-rond de jambe en l'air*) while bending the left leg. Immediately step (*piqué*) onto the right *demi-pointe* in second position and quickly close the left foot to fifth position front as the body makes one-half turn to the right. Continue turning to the right on both feet until facing the beginning direction once more, leaving the left

■ *Tour de basque*

65

BALLET TECHNIQUE:
CENTER WORK

foot in back in fifth position. Another turn can follow immediately to the same direction.

**Suggestions**   The crisp look of this turn is enhanced not only by the straight leg executing the *demi-rond de jambe* and *piqué* but also by the strong push from the floor and quick close to fifth position front by the second foot. As in *soutenu en tournant*, this turn is aided by the brisk closing of both arms from second position to a low, middle, or high position.

Preparatory Exercises

Before trying the turn, practice just the *demi-rond de jambe* and *piqué* to second position, closing the second foot quickly to fifth position front. Repeat the exercise immediately to the other side.

### *Tours Chaînés* (sheh-NAY)

**Definition**   Usually called simply *chaînés* ("chains, links"), these are a series of rapid, traveling turns, also known as *déboulés* ("rolling like a ball") or *petits tours*.

**Description**   *Chaînés* are small, rapid steps done in succession with a half-turn on each step, the feet close together in first position *en demi-pointes*. The turns travel across the floor, usually on a straight diagonal line. Momentum for the turns is initiated by the first step outward and opening of the arms to second position; immediately the pivot is made as the second foot closes to first position and the arms close either *en bas* or *en avant*. The energetic spotting of the eyes and snap of the head continues the momentum as the series of rapid half-turns travels across the room.

**Suggestions**   Keep the height of the *demi-pointes* position consistent and turn evenly on each foot, remembering that two equal half-turns make one full *chaîné* turn. Keep the hips and shoulders aligned so that the body turns as one unit, the legs straight and well turned out.

Preparatory Exercises

Make slow turning steps in second position, keeping the arms in second position for better balance. Concentrate on the spotting of the head toward a fixed point in the direction of the turns and on making *even* half-turns straight across the room. Later, turn with more speed, with the legs closer together (first position, heels almost touching), the arms low, and the path a diagonal from upstage left to downstage right, then from upstage right to downstage left. If balance is lost or proper direction cannot be maintained, walk quickly out of the line of traffic and, if possible, begin again.

## TURNS ON ONE FOOT

After becoming acquainted with the forementioned turns that are done on two feet, students usually are introduced to the following traveling turn in which the dancer steps directly onto one foot for the turn. It is helpful to analyze it in four sections: preparation, initiative, turn, and completion.

## *Piqué (or Posé) Tour en Dedans* (pee-kay TOOR ahn duh-DAHn)

**Preparation**   For a turn to the right, extend the right foot forward while making a *fondu* on the supporting leg. At the same time, turn the head toward the right shoulder and raise *en avant* the arm corresponding to the forward leg and the other arm to second position.

**Initiative**   Keeping the right leg straight with foot pointed, swing it to second position (as in a *demi-rond de jambe en dehors*) and, with a strong push from the supporting foot, immediately face the right leg and step directly onto *demi-pointe*, knee straight. At the same time, open the right arm slightly and raise the left foot *sur le cou-de-pied derrière* (in back of the right ankle) or to *retiré derrière* (behind, or just below, the back of the right knee).

■ *Piqué tour en dedans*

**Turn**   Without pause, execute a three-quarter turn *en dedans* to the right while closing the arms *en avant*. During the spin, the head faces briefly toward the left shoulder, then quickly resumes its focus over the right shoulder.

**Completion**   Lower the left foot into *fondu*, cutting directly under the right foot, and at the same time, quickly extend the right leg forward, keeping the knee straight and the toes only a few inches above the ground, and open the left arm to *second* position. The pose now is the same as the preparatory one.

The following turns occur in place, rather than traveling. Although the complete turn may not be included in most beginning classes, exercises to help achieve the strength, balance, and form for them are a part of first-year-class material. It is important to remember that a turn outward (*en dehors*) is in the direction of the raised leg; a turn inward (*en dedans*) is in the direction of the supporting leg.

## *Pirouettes* (peer-oo-ET)

### Preparatory Exercises

A series of *relevés* can be practiced facing the *barre*, with time allowed for balancing: From a *demi-plié* in second, fourth, or fifth positions, *relevé* onto the *demi-pointe* of one foot as the other foot lifts quickly to *retiré* position. A strong vertical lengthening down through the supporting *demi-pointe*, a level pelvis, and a well-turned-out *retiré* position are required. Close to a secure *demi-plié* in fifth position.

**Center floor exercises for *pirouettes en dehors*** To practice coordination of movements of the arms with the legs: *Pointe tendue à la seconde* with the right foot as the arms open to second position, close fifth position front in *demi-plié* as the right arm curves forward of the center of the body (*en avant*); with a push from both feet, *relevé* onto the left foot as the right foot lifts sharply to *retiré* position, left arm joining the right *en avant*. After the balance in this position, the feet return to fifth position *demi-plié* as the arms remain in place or open outward toward the audience. Later, a one-quarter turn outward in the direction of the raised leg can be made on each *relevé*, then half turns can follow.

**Center floor exercises for *pirouettes en dedans*** To practice coordination of movements of the arms with the legs: *Pointe tendue* forward toward downstage left with the right foot; *demi-plié* in fourth position, right arm *en avant* and left arm in second position; with a push from both feet, *relevé* onto the front (right) foot as the back (left) foot lifts sharply to *retiré* position, left arm joining the right *en avant*, and balance facing downstage right; close to fifth position *demi-plié*, left foot front.

■ Preparatory exercise for *pirouette en dehors* from fifth position (as seen from the front)

**Note**   The position of *retiré* for *pirouettes* varies in different schools of technique, but it usually is in front of the supporting leg with the pointed foot just below the knee. The preparatory *plié*, when taken in fourth position, also has variation; some schools prefer the back leg to remain straight, and only the front leg bent or *en fondu*.

## *Adage* (ah-DAHZH), *Adagio*

Always an important feature of center work, the *adage* is a series of movements combining *port de bras*, exercises from *barre* work (such as *pliés*, *relevés*, *battements*), center exercises (such as *développés* to any of the positions of the body) the line poses of *arabesque* and *attitude* — often linked by connecting movements such as *pas de bourrée* and *tombé* — and turns (usually not traveling but in place). These movements are done slowly and as though without effort, reflecting the Italian term *adagio* ("at ease" or "leisure"). The dancer must perform with coordination of the arms, legs, and head and with a flow of movement from one pose to another. Although the *adage* must look leisurely, it is a severe test of a dancer's balance, control, and strength. It can also be a test of memory.

Learn to observe and listen carefully as the *adage* is explained. As the movements are demonstrated, try to memorize them quickly or imitate them, using full movements of the arms but minimal physical effort in the legs so that the muscles do not overtire (this is called "marking" an exercise). Next will come the chance to perform the movements as completely as possible, or "full out." If the class is divided into groups, observe carefully as other groups work and learn from the corrections given them.

## NOTES

1. Agrippina Vaganova, *Basic Principles of Classical Ballet* (Leningrad, 1934), trans. Anatole Chujoy (New York: Dover, 1969), 44.

2. *Ibid.*

3. Carlo Blasis, *Code of Terpsichore* (London, 1828). Republished by Dance Horizons (New York, n.d.), 74.

4. *Ibid.*

5. Erik Bruhn and Lillian Moore, *Bournonville and Ballet Technique* (London: Adam & Charles Black, 1961), 42.

# CHAPTER 4

# BALLET TECHNIQUE: *ALLEGRO*

The lesson thus far has been a necessary prelude to the final, perhaps most important part — the *allegro* (ah-LEH-gro). Taken from the musical term, *allegro* in ballet means the brisk, often rapid, action steps that include jumps and the connecting, auxiliary movements. These lively steps have been called the "heart and soul of ballet," with their particular quality of elevation being its "crowning glory." The performance of *allegro* is a true test of a dancer's skill, unmistakably revealed in the classical variations (solo dances in a ballet that correspond to the arias of opera).

How a dancer travels across the floor or into the air is the subject of the following pages. But first, it may be helpful to think of ballet *allegro* in very general terms.

## FIVE FUNDAMENTAL MOVEMENTS OF ELEVATION

A dancer may spring

1. from both feet to both feet (the basis of *temps levé sauté*).
2. from both feet to one foot (the basis of *sissonne*).
3. from one foot to both feet (the basis of *assemblé*).
4. (or leap) from one foot to the other foot (the basis of *jeté*).
5. (or hop) on one foot (the basis of *temps levé*).

These basic movements are easiest to understand when they are done without extreme turnout of the legs. Although this procedure may sound unorthodox, it is meant only as an introduction and should lead quickly into the study of the specific steps (*pas*) of *allegro* as done from traditional ballet positions.

All jumps, leaps, and hops—whether from parallel or turned-out positions—require a bend of the knees (*plié*) for the push-off into the air and another *plié* after the jump to cushion the landing. In ballet, the landing *plié* from the first jump becomes the preparation for the next jump, thus linking the jumps together rather like the bounces of a ball. The knees and insteps of the feet act as springs; the jumps appear light and bouncy as though done from a springboard. This bouncy quality, known as *ballon* (bah-LOHn), gives the dancer the appearance of being airborne rather than earthbound. Indeed, in steps of very high elevation, the dancer seems to be suspended momentarily in flight. Good *ballon* often takes years to achieve, but some of the following exercises can give even the beginning student a sense of rebound from the floor. They are primarily offered, however, to introduce the five fundamental movements of elevation.

### Exercises

(1) *Springs from both feet to both feet:* With the legs parallel (or with a very slight turnout), take very small jumps in place. The feet need not point fully, but the landing from each jump must be very soft, going through the toes, to the balls of the feet, to the heels as the knees bend directly over the feet. This landing is fundamental to all the jumps that follow.

(2) and (3) *Springs from both feet to one foot and from one foot to both feet:* With legs parallel (or with a very slight turnout), bend the knees and push off from two feet, landing on one foot; spring from that foot onto both. Do a series of these movements traveling across the room, forward or backward, as well as in place and alternating sides. (Most *allegro* steps can be done in many different directions.)

(4) *Leaps from one foot to the other foot:* Take a slow run or lope across the room. Notice that the landing of the foot is from toe to heel, not heel to toe. This is true of all landings in *allegro*. Try to lope higher, covering less space forward but more space vertically.

(5) *Hops on one foot:* These can be done in the same way as exercise 1 but on one foot, for a series of small hops, before changing to the other foot. They also can be done as a step-hop (a skip) across the floor, either forward or backward, with the arms swinging naturally. Try for higher elevation, with the knee of the bent leg lifted high in front and the other leg straight, the toes of both feet fully pointed in the air.

Combining these basic movements can quickly give a beginning student an introduction to *allegro* combinations, which later will form much of the work in the center. A sample combination of basic movements might be three leaps forward (on the right, on the left, on the right), hop on the right, spring to both feet, spring to one foot, spring to both feet, spring to one foot. The combination should take eight counts and it could be repeated across the floor. In an as yet unrefined way, the student is doing essentially: *jeté, jeté, jeté, temps levé, assemblé, sissonne, assemblé, sissonne.*

One hopes the student also is sensing some of the quality of *ballon* and the pleasure of moving across the floor to a musical phrase and along with other people.

## BASIC JUMPS

The first steps of elevation to be learned are basic jumps, which begin from and end on both feet — *temps levé sauté, soubresaut, changement de pieds*, and *échappé sauté*. These, and most other *allegro* steps, are best learned at the *barre* before they are attempted in the center floor. In many cases there are preliminary exercises that can precede the performance of the actual step — a kind of evolution helpful to the final understanding. The following general points should be kept in mind when performing these four jumps.

The preparatory movement must be a good *demi-plié* — knees bent directly over the feet and as deeply as the Achilles tendons will allow; the feet firmly on the ground at the big toes, little toes, and heels; the hips, ribs, shoulders, and head poised in perfect alignment. From the *demi-plié*, there is a strong push-off from the floor — the thigh muscles contract, and the knees straighten as the feet leave the floor by a firm push through the insteps and toes. In the air, the body is in alignment, abdominal muscles lengthened upward, the feet fully arched. The landing from the jump must be smooth; do not anticipate the floor by relaxing the points of the feet until the toes just touch the ground, then roll down through the balls and soles of the feet to the heels, allowing the knees to bend into the *demi-plié* and keeping the pelvis from tilting forward. When the jumps first are attempted, the arms usually are carried low — in first position or *demi-seconde*, sometimes in second position and always supported from the center of the back. In most instances, the timing of the jump requires that the dancer be in the air on count *and*, then return to the ground on count *1*.

All *allegro* steps that follow are illustrated as seen *from the back*. The illustrated sequences read from left to right.

### Temps Levé Sauté (tahn leh-vay soh-TAY)
**Definition**   Literally, the term means "raised jumped movement." The movement is simply a spring from both feet ending in the same position.
**Description**   This jump is learned in first position, later in second. The elements of the step are *demi-plié* in first position (or second); push directly upward into the air; land in *demi-plié* as in the starting position.

> Preparatory Exercise
>
> *Relevés* finishing in *demi-plié* (see Chapter 2, "*Plié*") done in first and second positions are basic to the understanding of *temps levés sautés* in those positions.

■ *Temps levé sauté* in first position

**Other Forms**   The exercise and the jump may be done in all positions of the feet and with simple variation in arm positions.

### *Soubresaut* (soo-bruh-SOH)

**Definition**   This step is aptly named: *soubre* ("sudden") *saut* ("jump or jumping"). It is, in effect, a *temps levé sauté* performed in fifth position.

**Description**   From *demi-plié* in fifth position, push directly upward into the air with the feet tightly crossed so that no space shows between the legs; land

■ *Soubresaut*

in *demi-plié* as in the starting position (the foot that began in front also finishes front).

Preparatory Exercise

Springing *relevés* done from fifth position (*sous-sus*) can introduce the tightly crossed position of the feet on the *demi-pointes*. In *soubresaut* the position is the same, except that in the air the toes can be pointed.

**Other Forms**   Although the basic *soubresaut* is done in place, the step also can be done traveling slightly forward, backward, or sideward. The body moves as one compact unit, propelled by the directional push from the feet.

### Changement de Pieds (shahnzh-mahn duh pee-AY)

**Definition**   Meaning "change of feet," this term usually is shortened to *changement*. It is a spring from fifth position to fifth position, landing with the foot that was in front now in back.

**Description**   From fifth position, right foot front, *demi-plié* and push into the air, opening the legs slightly to first position; land in fifth position *demi-plié* with the left foot front (taking care that the feet do not overcross the fifth position at the finish of the *changement*).

**Other Forms**   *Changements* can turn in the air at the moment of the jump. They are done as quarter turns, beginning in the direction of the foot that was in front, with the body turning as one unit and the eyes focusing clearly in each new direction.

■ *Changement de pieds*

*Petits changements* are those in which the toes barely leave the floor during the jump, the action happening more from the arches and ankles than from the knees and thighs.

*Grands changements* are very high jumps done with the legs thrown apart (*écarté*). Also known as *ciseaux* because of their scissor-like quality, *grands changements* are practiced at later stages of technical training.

### Échappé Sauté (ay-shah-PAY soh-TAY)

**Definition**   In this jump, the feet escape from a closed position to an open one, thus reflecting the meaning of the term — "escaped movement jumped."

■ *Grand échappé sauté à la seconde*

**Description** In *petit échappé sauté*, the jump is not high but simply a small spring from a *demi-plié* in fifth position to a *demi-plié* in second position. The step is completed with another small springing jump returning to fifth position, usually finishing with the foot that began in front now in back.

The *grand échappé sauté* is a larger jump requiring more skill: From a *demi-plié* in fifth position, spring high into the air with the legs close together and feet well crossed as in *soubresaut*, arms *en avant*; open the legs and arms to second position in the air, then land in a strong second position *demi-plié* with the ankles well supported and thighs well turned out; spring again into the air, the legs in second position; draw the legs together before landing in fifth position *demi-plié*, usually finishing with the foot that began in front now in back and arms *en bas*.

**Other Forms** *Échappés sautés* can be done to fourth position as well as second and with a finish on one foot in *fondu* instead of the return to fifth position *demi-plié*.

*Échappés relevés* are done to the *demi-pointes*, without the spring into the air, as described in Chapter 2, "*Élevé/Relevé*."

## MORE COMPLEX JUMPS: *PETIT ALLEGRO* STEPS

The following *allegro* steps, although considered elementary, require more co-ordination and considerable strength. They have many forms from simple to complex, and thus they are practiced in every level of ballet class, from beginner to professional. Before discussing the basic forms of these steps, it is wise to review some terms that will be used in describing them. Here the "gesture" foot refers to the foot that is the first to rise, open, or otherwise leave the original position:

*Dessus* (duh-SUI): The gesture foot passes over (in front of) the supporting foot.

*Dessous* (duh-SOO): The gesture foot passes under (in back of) the supporting foot.

*Devant* (duh-VAHn): The gesture foot begins from and ends in the front.

*Derrière* (deh-reeAIR): The gesture foot begins from and ends in the back.

*En avant* (ah-na-VAHn): The step is executed in a direction forward, toward the audience.

*En arrière* (ah-na-reeAIR): The step is executed in a direction backward, away from the audience.

### *Sissonne* (see-SAWN)
**Definition** *Sissonne* is a spring from both feet that finishes on one foot, and as such it represents the second half of a compound step called *pas de sissonne*

■ *Sissonne ouverte de coté*

in eighteenth-century dance technique. Today, if the gesture leg remains extended after the landing, it is a *sissonne ouverte* (oo-VAIRT), or open. When a quick return to fifth position is required, it is a *sissonne fermée* (fair-MAY), or closed.

**Description**   The most elementary form is *sissonne simple* (SAn-pluh) and is performed like a *soubresaut* but with a finish on one foot in *fondu*, the other foot pointed just above the supporting ankle, either in front (*devant*) or in back (*derrière*).

Most other forms typically travel sideward, forward, or backward and may finish *ouverte* or *fermée*. The body moves as one unit, the torso and arms established in a secure design during the spring and the landing. The following *sissonnes* travel to the side (*de coté*) with the gesture leg opening *à la seconde* at half height (*à la demi-hauteur*):

> *Sissonne ouverte de coté*: From fifth position, right foot front, *demi-plié* and spring into the air from both feet, traveling slightly sideward in the direction of the front foot as the back leg extends *à la seconde*; land on the right foot in *fondu*. Pause in this position with the left leg remaining raised, then close by sliding the foot through *pointe tendue* to fifth position.

> *Sissonne fermée dessus*: Perform as above, but after landing in *fondu*, quickly slide the left foot to the fifth position front.

> *Sissonne fermée dessous*: Travel sideward on the *sissonne* in the direction of the back foot, quickly close the gesture foot behind in fifth position.

**Other Forms**   Both *sissonne ouverte* and *fermée* may travel forward or backward in various positions of the body. A particularly pleasing version is *sissonne ouverte* traveling forward (*en avant*) in an *arabesque*. (See Chapter 3, "Arabesque," for various *arabesque* positions.)

Shown in third *arabesque*, Russian school

## *Assemblé* (ah-sah*n*-BLAY)

**Definition**   This is a spring off of one foot onto both feet. The term means "assembled" and refers to the bringing together of the legs in the air so that the landing can be made on both feet simultaneously.

**Description**   *Assemblé dessus*: From fifth position, right foot back, brush the right foot to the side as the supporting knee bends deeply; without pause continue the *dégagé* movement until the right foot is off the floor; push strongly from the floor with the supporting leg, maximizing the stretch of both legs in the air and the pointing of both feet; assemble the legs in the air by bringing the right leg in front of the left; alight simultaneously on both feet in *demi-plié*, right foot front in fifth position. An opening of the arms outward from the body, motivated by a sense of breath in the torso, helps achieve the lightness required in this step.

The following variations are described only briefly, the essential action of the legs remaining the same as in the *assemblé dessus*.

*Assemblé dessous:* The front foot brushes to the side and closes in back.

*Assemblé devant:* The front foot brushes to the side and returns to the front.

*Assemblé derrière:* The back foot brushes to the side and returns to the back.

*Assemblé en avant:* The front foot brushes forward and returns to the front.

*Assemblé en arrière:* The back foot brushes backward and returns to the back.

The *assemblés en avant* and *en arrière* require somewhat greater control, especially of the spine, and therefore are usually the last of this series to be learned.

### Preparatory Exercise

As a preparation for *assemblé dessus*, from fifth position, right foot back, *dégagé* to the side with the back foot as the supporting knee bends. *Relevé* high on the supporting foot, close the right foot front and *demi-plié* on both feet in fifth position. From that same *demi-plié*, begin the exercise with the left foot brushing to the side, and so forth. Reverse the entire action as a preparation for *assemblé dessous*. The other *assemblés* can benefit from similar exercises, learned at the *barre*. As center exercises they are particularly challenging.

**Other Forms**    *Assemblé porté* ("carried") is an *assemblé* that travels in the direction of the gesture leg, motivated by the impetus of that leg.

*Assemblé coupé* ("cut") occurs when the weight is already on one foot, the other foot in a position off the floor such as *sur le cou-de-pied derrière* following a *sissonne simple*.

*Grand assemblé* is performed with the gesture leg brushing to full height, or *à la hauteur*, which is parallel to the floor.

### Temps Levé (tahn luh-VAY)

**Definition**    *Temps levé*, meaning "movement (or time) raised," is a hop on one foot with the other foot raised and held in any given position, unlike the *temps levé sauté*, which is a jump from both feet.

**Description**    Usually in the beginning classes, the raised foot is placed just above the ankle of the supporting foot, either in front (*sur le cou-de-pied devant*) or in back (*sur le cou-de-pied derrière*). The ankle of the raised leg is fully extended and the toes pointed. From a strong *fondu*, the supporting leg pushes from the floor with elevation high enough for it to fully straighten, foot arched and toes pointed downward. The return to the ground is to that same leg, lowering smoothly into *fondu*.

Preparatory Exercises

*Fondus* and *relevés*, with the raised foot *sur le cou-de-pied devant* or *derrière*, can be incorporated in *barre* exercises to prepare for *temps levé*. They first should be practiced slowly, then with gradually increased speed, but always in moderation. Both this exercise and the *allegro* step are strenuous.

**Other Forms**   The position of the raised leg can determine the name of variations of this step, for instance, *temps levé en arabesque* and *temps levé en retiré* (discussed later in this chapter).

In the Cecchetti method, *temps levé* also can refer to a spring from fifth position finishing with one foot raised *sur le cou-de-pied* (*sissonne simple*, in other methods).

## *Jeté* (zhuh-TAY)

**Definition**   *Jeté* means "thrown." It is a spring or leap from one foot to the other, done with a strong brush or "throw" of the leg into the air.

**Description**   The most basic small *jetés* are the following two:

*Jeté dessus*: From fifth position, right foot back, *demi-plié* and brush the back foot into the air as in a strong *battement dégagé à la seconde* while keeping the supporting leg in *fondu*; immediately spring upward so that for a

■ *Jeté dessus*

moment both legs are straight and both feet are pointed in the air; land in *fondu* on the right foot just in front of the spot vacated by the supporting foot, which now points just above and in back of the right ankle. To continue in a series, brush the back (left) foot into the air from its pointed position at the ankle.

*Jeté dessous*: Perform as above, but brush the front foot to the side and finish the step with it in back, the other foot pointed just above and in front of the ankle.

The direction of movement for *jetés dessus* and *dessous* is up; they are thrown directly upward into the air and do not travel from side to side, even though the weight is transferred from one foot to the other on each *jeté*.

### Preparatory Exercise

A preparation for *jeté dessus*: From fifth position, right foot back, *dégagé* the back foot to the side while bending the supporting knee, *relevé* on the supporting foot, bring the right foot momentarily to fifth position front, and immediately lower onto it in *fondu*. When the transfer of weight is made, the left foot arches just above and behind the right ankle. Continue in the same manner, brushing the left foot to the side from its pointed position (now more like the action of a *battement frappé*). Reverse the entire action as a preparation for *jetés dessous*.

**Other Forms**   *Jeté en avant* travels forward, initiated by a strong *dégagé* to the front. *Jeté en arrière* travels backward, with the *dégagé* brushing to the back.

The large *jeté* step, or *grand jeté*, is more appropriately a part of *grand allegro* (discussed later in this chapter).

## Pas de Chat (pah duh SHAH)

**Definition**   The term means "step of the cat" and implies the quick, catlike springing movement from one foot to the other, characteristic of this step.

**Description**   Of the several styles of this step, the most elementary are the following versions, all of which travel directly sideward.

> *Petit pas de chat:* From fifth position, right foot back, *demi-plié* and briskly raise the back foot, arched, to the ankle of the left foot; immediately spring upward and to the side, quickly raising the left foot so that the toes of both feet almost touch in the air; land in *fondu* on the right foot and quickly close the left foot to fifth position front in *demi-plié*. The body should incline slightly in the direction of movement.

> *Grand pas de chat:* Perform exactly as above, but raise the feet to the height of the knee (*retiré* position) and spring higher into the air with a sharp action from the thighs. Maintain a strong turnout, especially during the closing of the second leg into a secure fifth position *demi-plié*.

## ADDITIONAL *ALLEGRO* STEPS

Each of the following steps contains three transfers of weight, usually each shift of weight occurring on each beat of a 3/4 measure of music, such as a waltz rhythm. Related versions of these steps are found in some folk dances.

## Balancé (bah-lahn-SAY)

**Definition**   The verb *balancer* can mean "to swing or rock to and fro." The *pas balancé* has three steps, with a shift of weight on each step, usually performed in a waltz rhythm.

83

**Description**  *Balancé* is a step of many moods: Sometimes it is bouncy and performed with a light *jeté*; other times it is romantic and performed with a low glide along the floor. In all *balancés*, the legs must remain very turned out, and the lowering to *fondu* must be done softly. The following version is done *de côté* ("to the side") and usually begins with the back foot:

> *Balancé de côté:* From fifth position, right foot back, *demi-plié* and extend the right foot to the side; with a slight spring, *tombé* over onto the right foot, bringing the left foot directly behind the right ankle (*sur le cou-de-pied derrière*); shift the weight onto the left *demi-pointe*, bringing the right foot just off the ground; *fondu* in place on the right foot, arching the left foot behind the right ankle (*sur le cou-de-pied derrière*). The *balancé* can now be repeated to the left side.

Movements of the arms (*ports de bras*) coordinated with movements of the head and shoulders (*épaulements*) can add a smooth, lyrical quality to the *balancé*.

**Other Forms**  *Balancés* may be performed *en avant* or *en arrière* ("forward" or "backward") in various positions of the body. They may be done *en tournant*, completing one half-turn on each *balancé*.

### *Pas de Basque* (pah duh BAHSK)
**Definition**  The "Basque step," commonly found in folk dances of almost every country, takes its name from the Basques, a people of the Pyrenees region of southern France and northern Spain. In its simplest form, it is not unlike the

*balancé*, except that after the first step to the side, the movement is always forward or backward.

**Description**    The *pas de basque* frequently begins facing one downstage corner and finishes to the other. It has many forms: It may be jumped or glided, large or small, or it may turn. A variety of *port de bras* can be used in the following versions:

> *Pas de basque sauté en avant:* From the fifth position, right foot front, *demi-plié* and, with the right foot, execute a *demi-rond de jambe en dehors* (that is, extend the foot forward and then to the side) slightly above the floor; spring to the side onto the right foot, bringing the left foot arched in front of the right ankle (*sur le cou-de-pied devant*); step forward to *croisé* onto the left foot, close to fifth position or *coupé dessous* with the right foot, arching the left foot in front of the supporting ankle (*sur le cou-de-pied devant*). The *pas de basque* now can be repeated to the left side. All movements can be reversed to perform the *pas de basque sauté en arrière*.

> *Pas de basque glissé en avant:* From fifth position, right foot front, *demi-plié* and, with the right foot, execute a *demi-rond de jambe en dehors à terre* and immediately shift the weight onto the right foot in *fondu*, extending the left foot *pointe tendue à la seconde*; slide the left foot through first position *demi-plié* (some styles like it also to slide into fifth position) and forward into fourth position, taking care that the legs remain well turned out and the ankles supported, and remain in *demi-plié*; shift the weight onto the left foot as both legs straighten; slide the right foot into fifth position behind in *demi-plié*. The *pas de basque* can now be repeated to the left side, or all movements reversed for *pas de basque glissé en arrière*.

85

■ *Pas de basque glissé en avant*

*Pas de basque glissé* can be useful as a preparatory step leading into another movement or as a connecting step between two other movements. Other such linking steps are described next.

## CONNECTING STEPS: PREPARATORY MOVEMENTS

Jumps are not always done one right after another. Instead, they often are linked together by connecting steps. Because they are done close to the ground, these steps give contrast to the high jump that will follow and serve as a preparation for and introduction to the more exciting step. The connecting steps have another purpose — to carry the dancer from one spot to another. When done in a series and with *épaulement*, these relatively small and simple movements have a charm of their own.

### *Glissade* (glee-SAHD)

**Definition**   Meaning "to glide," *glissade* is done close to the ground, with a brush of one foot along the floor, a shift of weight to that foot, and a slide into fifth position by the other foot. *Glissade* is considered a *terre à terre* ("ground-to-ground") step, because the feet barely leave the floor.

**Description**   The following *glissades* travel to the side, beginning and ending with the same foot in front. The feet must not be lifted high off the floor, even though at one moment both legs are straight and both feet are fully pointed. The entire action of the step is timed *and 1*, with the close to fifth position on count *1*. Performance should be light, with care taken to control the turnout, especially of the closing leg, so that the knees are well open and arches supported in the fifth position *demi-plié*.

*Glissade derrière:* From fifth position, right foot back, *demi-plié* and extend the back foot along the floor to the side, finishing with the foot fully arched and toes pointed a few inches off the floor, the left leg remaining in *fondu*; with a slight spring, shift the weight to the right leg in *fondu*, extending the left leg as the left foot points just slightly off the floor; quickly slide the left foot into fifth position front in *demi-plié*.

*Glissade devant:* Perform as above but begin with the front foot, which remains in front at the close.

In the following *glissades*, the basic action and timing of the legs are the same as above, but they are done with a change of feet (sometimes called *glissades changées*, especially when done in a series):

■ *Glissade derrière*

*Glissade dessous:* Travel to the side, leading with the front foot, which finishes in back.

*Glissade dessus:* Travel to the side, leading with the back foot, which finishes in front.

### Preparatory Exercise

To learn the *glissade*, break the step down into four slow parts: From fifth position, *demi-plié* (count 1), extend one foot along the floor while the other leg remains in *fondu* (count 2), shift the weight onto the leading foot into *fondu* and close to fifth position *demi-plié* (count and 3), straighten the knees (count 4).

**Other Forms**   *Glissades* also may travel forward or backward *en face* or on the diagonals in *croisé* or *effacé*. The basic action and timing remain the same:

*Glissade en arrière:* Travel backward, leading with the back foot, which finishes in back.

*Glissade en avant:* Travel forward, leading with the front foot, which finishes in front.

Any of the above versions may be performed as an *adagio glissade*, that is, done more slowly, often with the transfer of weight on count 1 and the closing on count 2. Important here is the smooth transition, *legato* in quality, often used to link movements and poses in an *adage* combination. (See Chapter 3, "*Adage, Adagio.*")

## *Coupé* (koo-PAY)

**Definition**   *Coupé* means "cut." As a step it has many forms, all involving one foot "cutting away" the other in order to replace it. Usually this occurs as a preparation for another step, but sometimes *coupés* are performed in a series from one foot to the other.

**Description**   *Coupés* are done *dessous* (one foot cutting under) or *dessus* (one foot cutting over) to replace the supporting foot. This may be done with a spring into the air or with a rise to the *demi-pointes*.

*Coupé dessous sauté: Fondu* on the right foot as the left foot arches just above and in back of the right ankle. Spring into the air just high enough to allow the right foot to arch, toes pointing downward, and land on the left foot in *fondu*, right foot arched just above and in front of the left ankle (*sur le cou-de-pied devant*). The action is reversed for *coupé dessus*, the front foot cutting over the back foot that immediately arches *sur le cou-de-pied derrière*.

*Coupé dessous par terre:* From *pointe tendue* fourth position back, *fondu* on the supporting leg. Sharply draw the back foot to fifth position on the

■ *Coupé dessous par terre*

*demi-pointes*; *fondu* on the back leg as the front foot extends to fourth position front at *pointe tendue* or slightly off the ground. This version also can be reversed for *coupé dessus*, in which case the front foot cuts over the back foot. As an alternate method, the leg can open with a small *développé* from the fifth position.

## *Chassé* (shah-SAY) *en l'Air*
**Definition**  Performed as a sliding movement, *chassés* ("chased") give the appearance of one foot chasing the other from its position. The term also is used for a *terre à terre* connecting movement made by a slide of the foot from fifth position *demi-plié* to second or fourth position (see "*Glissé*," Chapter 3).

■ *Chassé en l'air en avant*

**Description**    *Chassés* are done with a smooth sliding motion, achieved by leading into the slide with the toes rather than the heel, the latter causing a galloping quality instead.

> *Chassé en l'air en avant:* Facing a downstage corner, *demi-plié* in fifth position, right foot front. Spring into the air, alight on the left foot in *fondu* with the right foot arched in front of the supporting ankle, the toes close to the ground. Immediately slide the right foot forward to fourth position, transferring the weight to the right leg in *fondu* as the left leg extends, foot pointing on, or close to, the ground. To repeat, spring forward into the air, immediately closing the left leg behind the right, alight in *fondu* on the left foot, and continue as above.

These movements sometimes are called *temps levé chassé.*

Preparatory Exercise

Before attempting *chassés en l'air*, it is helpful to practice the movements as described above, but with *relevés* instead of springs into the air.

**Other Forms**    The dancer can slide into fourth position *demi-plié*, rather than transferring the weight on through to a *fondu* on the forward leg, and then continue as above. Frequently this method is used for *chassés à la seconde*, with the slide into a second position *demi-plié* rather than a *fondu*. The foot that follows, or chases, always closes behind the leading foot.

Moving backward in *chassés en arrière* is the most challenging: after the preparatory spring, land on the front foot and slide the back foot backward to fourth position *demi-plié* or *fondu*. The chasing action is then made by the front foot each time.

## ADDITIONAL CONNECTING STEPS AND PREPARATORY MOVEMENTS

Many connecting movements appropriate to use with *allegro* steps also are used with slower center work, as in a sequence of *adagio* movements. These include steps already discussed in the previous chapter, such as *glissé, tombé, piqué,* and, especially, various *pas de bourrées.* Another variation of *pas de bourrée,* useful as a preparatory step leading into a *grand allegro* step, is the following.

### Pas de Bourrée Couru or Pas Couru (koo-REW)

**Definition**  *Pas couru* ("run") resembles a *pas de bourrée* because it is a compound movement made up of three quick steps, in this case performed as a smooth run.

**Description**  To perform *pas de bourrée couru,* or *pas couru, en avant*: From a *pointe tendue croisé derrière* with the right foot, *fondu* on the front (left) leg as the right makes a small *développé* forward; with a push from the *fondu,* step

■ *Pas de bourrée couru en avant*

well forward onto the right foot, quickly descending through the instep, and then forward onto the left foot; without pause, step out again onto the right foot, this time into *fondu* as the impetus for the ensuing *allegro* step.

The three forward steps (right, left, right) occur quickly without interruption as a three-step run, the final step having the strongest bend or *fondu*. All the running steps are done with the toes descending first, not the heels, and with the body well forward toward the direction of the run. As the run begins, the arms can open outward to help start the momentum, then close quickly before the final step in order to extend in a desired position that enhances the *grand allegro* movement that follows.

## *GRAND ALLEGRO* STEPS

*Grand* ("large") *allegro* steps require more strength and cover more space, both into the air and across the floor, than the preceding ones. Thus, they are practiced after basic principles of *petit allegro* are understood, when the body is thoroughly warmed up, and usually toward the end of class. Probably no *allegro* step is more fun to do or more exciting to watch than the following.

### *Grand Jeté en Avant* (grahn zhuh-TAY ah-na-VAHn)
**Definition**   This is a large leap traveling forward, preceded by a preparatory step such as *pas couru* or *chassé* to give the necessary impetus.

■ *Grand jeté en avant*

**Description**   After an appropriate preparatory step, one that finishes in a *fondu* on the forward leg with the torso reaching upward and slightly forward, thrust the back leg forward into a strong *grand battement devant*, propelling the body into the air by the push-off from the other leg, which is then thrust upward into a *grand battement derrière*. Both feet and legs are extended completely in the air, the body momentarily weightlessly airborne in a suspended pose.

Alight in the same pose, with the back leg and foot remaining extended in *arabesque* as the leading foot releases sufficiently to allow a deep *fondu* on the supporting leg. The torso, which has remained quietly lifted during the leap, is allowed to tip slightly forward from the pelvis upon landing in order to balance over the center of the supporting foot.

As a general rule, alignment of the shoulders with the rest of the torso is easier to maintain if the arms are extended in second *arabesque* rather than first. Therefore, *grands jetés* done with opposition—for example, if the right leg executes the *grand battement en avant*, the left arm is brought forward—are the most effective for early attempts. The fingers of the forward hand should be just above eye level, and the eyes focused at some point slightly higher.

### *Temps Levé en Arabesque* (tahn luh-VAY ah na-ra-BESK)

**Definition**   This is a hop or spring on one foot, with the other leg extended in *arabesque*, and is sometimes called *arabesque sautée*.

**Description**   To perform in first *arabesque*: Stand with the weight well centered over the right leg, the left leg extended straight behind at the desired *arabesque* height, the right arm extended forward, and the left arm opened to the side; without otherwise altering the pose, *fondu* on the right leg and push

■ *Temps levé en arabesque*

from the right foot into the air, quickly pointing the right foot and completely extending the leg; alight on the right foot in a controlled *fondu*, maintaining the pose of first *arabesque*.

To perform a series of *temps levé* on the same leg, step forward on the left leg and then forward into a *fondu* on the right leg to begin the action as described above. To alternate legs, precede each *temps levé* with a *pas couru* (three running steps) or simply execute as a step hop on the right leg and then a step hop on the left. Alternate the arms by passing them through the *en avant* position.

### Temps Levé en Retiré (tahn luh-VAY ahn ruh-tih-RAY)

**Definition**   A spring or hop is made on one foot with the other foot drawn up to *retiré* position.

**Description**   To perform in *retiré derrière*: Stand in *croisé* on the left foot with the right foot pointed behind the supporting knee and the right thigh well turned out, the arms established in a desired position; *fondu*, push into the air, and alight as described above for *temps levé en arabesque* but in the *retiré* pose.

To perform in a series on the same leg, step forward on the right leg and then forward into a *fondu* on the left leg to begin the *temps levé* action once again. To alternate legs, follow the general procedures described above for *temps levé en arabesque*.

■ Temps levé en retiré

## *ALLEGRO* COMBINATIONS

When several different steps are joined together to be performed to a musical phrase, it is called a combination or *enchaînement* (ahn-shain-MAHn), literally, a "linking." *Allegro* combinations are the student's first taste of what it may be to dance—to perform one step after another, in time to music, with a definite beginning, middle, and ending of a movement and musical phrase.

A combination, indeed any single step, requires coordinated arm and head movements if it is to be more than mere physical drill. Beginners learn the basic small jumps with the arms carried simply *en bas*, or in first position, the head straight. At that stage of learning, it is important to train the upper body, head, and arms not to react to the movement of the legs; flapping arms, jiggling shoulders, and a seesaw spine are to be avoided from the very beginning. But in steps such as *glissade* or *assemblé*, where the legs open out from the body, the beginner should open the arms also, usually to *demi-seconde*.

Later, steps of high elevation such as *grand échappé sauté*, large *assemblés*, or *sissonnes* benefit from arms (*not* shoulders) that rise to higher positions as the height of the jump is reached. A change of focus for the head and eyes, the use of *épaulement*, and the use of different directions of the body also add interest to *allegro* combinations in subsequent stages of training. Such coordination requires great skill and is the result of many classes, great patience, and determination to try and try and try, and then try once again.

## BEATS

The broad term for steps with beats is *batterie* (bat-REE). Although classes in basic ballet do not include steps with beats, students in those classes may be curious about what is meant by "beats."

Once basic *allegro* steps are mastered, many of them are embellished, and some are performed exclusively with beats. These include such small steps as the *entrechats* ("braidings or interweavings")—jumps with rapid crossings of the legs in the air, *petite batterie*. The beats are made as the calves of the legs open out and close in, crossing in front and behind each other. Since both legs are active in movement, they are both counted; for example, in an *entrechat quatre*, because each leg makes two crossings, the step counts as four (*quatre*) beats. A few dancers (male) have managed five crossings—an *entrechat dix*. An uneven number, as in *entrechat trois* (three), usually indicates a finish on one foot or in an open position (second or fourth).

Beaten steps requiring higher elevation, *grande batterie*, include the *cabrioles* ("capers"), in which one leg is thrown into the air followed by the underneath leg, which beats against it, sending the first leg even higher into the air.

One of the best preparations for *batterie* is the following exercise.

## TEMPS LEVÉS SAUTÉS BATTUS EN SECONDE

(tah*n* leh-VAY soh-TAY bah-TEW zahn suh-GOH*n*D)

**Definition**   A series of jumps in second position taken with a beat of the legs before each landing.

**Description**   To prepare for *grande batterie*: *Demi-plié* in second position and push high into the air, fully stretching the legs and arching the feet; at the height of the jump, and with the legs well turned out, beat the calves together, right leg in front; open both legs and land in second position *demi-plié*. Repeat, beating with the left leg front. Continue for a series of *sautés*, alternating beats in this manner.

To prepare for rapid *petite batterie*: *Demi-plié* in a smaller second position and spring slightly off the ground, extending the legs and sharply arching the feet, but not necessarily completely straightening the knees; immediately bring the legs together, crossing the right foot well in front so that both heels are visible as the legs beat from the base of the calves downwards; open both legs and land in a small second position *demi-plié*. Continue in a series, alternating the leg that beats in front.


## RÉVÉRENCE (ray-vay-RAH*n*s)

The ballet class may end with a last flourish of jumps, or it may conclude with slow *pliés*, *relevés*, *grands battements*, or *port de bras* to allow the students to wind down after working vigorously for an hour or more. In either case, the final movement of class is often the *révérence*, a bow or curtsy taken by teacher and class in appreciation of their mutual effort.

A *révérence* may range in form from simple to elaborate. For a woman, it is often a step to the side as the arms open to second position; the other foot is then brought behind the supporting foot, and the knees bend as the body leans slightly forward from the hips. A man may simply step forward, bringing the other foot close with the knee relaxed, arms remaining at the side as the head bows forward.

The *révérence* taken in class is not unlike the one a performer may take in acknowledgment of applause. Indeed, there is even applause after the class *révérence*, whereby the students formally thank the instructor and the accompanist for the lesson.

## POSTSCRIPT

These, then, are some of the fundamentals of ballet technique — to be learned by the beginner and to be practiced daily by the aspiring dancer. Words and drawings can help analyze the mechanics of movements, but they are meager tools when it comes to communicating the *sensation* of a movement, the way it *feels*. Some people believe that mental images can help students toward a deeper sensation and understanding. For instance, a *plié* could be imagined as starting, not just from the thighs, but very high in the center of the torso, so that the action is sensed as a slow opening of the body, right down the middle, into two equal halves. (This "halving" is easier to sense when a student stands between two *barres* or chairs, one hand holding onto each.) As another example, when a leg is lifted, as in *grand battement* to the front, one could imagine that the force for the *battement* comes from deep within the body down the back of the leg, thus throwing the leg lightly into the air. Or, the *grand battement* could be sensed as though a string were pulled tightly and then released slowly to allow the leg to descend smoothly.

The visual excitement of watching a truly fine dancer comes, ultimately, from the dancer's look of oneness with the movement. Steps do not seem pasted on but as though they grew outward from the very core of the dancer. Tamara Karsavina, famous ballerina with the Diaghilev Ballets Russes and then revered teacher, offered this advice to students:

> Do not discard your "feel" of the movement as you do your practice tunic at the end of the class. Take it with you on the bus or the train; there is no extra fare for it. Remember that the mechanism of the dance becomes artistry only when it is inspired by feeling and that feeling perpetuated in your mind will pass into your movements.[1]

## NOTE

1. Tamara Karsavina, *Classical Ballet: The Flow of Movement* (London: Adam & Charles Black, 1962), 15.

# CHAPTER 5
# THE BALLET BODY

The studio mirror reflects many shapes and sizes, but seldom a perfect ballet physique—and this has always been true. Many a dancer has succeeded as a fine performer despite having a less than ideal body. For any dancer, "talent" really translates into effective use of one's own individual body construction in order to maximize its actual capabilities. Discovering and developing these capabilities, including one's mental capacities, are very real joys of dance training, regardless of other goals.

## THE IDEAL PHYSIQUE

When the goal is a professional career as a ballet dancer, then specific physical requirements usually must be met, for both aesthetic and practical fitness purposes. Ballet aesthetics, the rules and principles of beautifully balanced forms in space, translates for the dancer as the ability of the body to create a beautiful line. A body that has well-balanced proportions and long, slender limbs will therefore be an asset. Practical ballet fitness, the body's capacity to perform the particular skills required in ballet technique, means the dancer's body must be able to function reliably during a demanding dance regimen. This, too, is better met by a well-proportioned body because it

> . . . will weather the stresses and strains of the exacting work required of it with greater ease than one in which there is some disparity in the relative length, for instance, of limbs to torso, of width to length of the body, or the relative size of shoulders to hips and so on. . . . Moreover, in the well-formed, well-proportioned

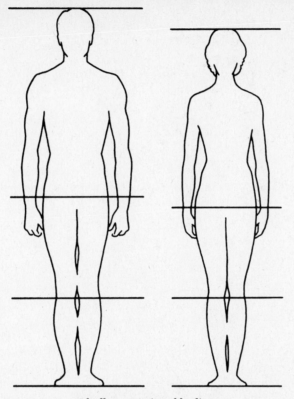

**Ideally proportioned bodies**

physique there is less likelihood of muscles thickening in unwanted places, and less proneness to the minor and sometimes major mishaps caused by the effort to overcome obstacles which are inherent in the build of the body.[1]

Ballet dancers need a certain flexibility — in the spine in order to achieve an *arabesque* line and a fluid carriage of the arms; in the hip joints for maximum turnout and extension of the legs; and in the ankles and feet for quick, articulate *allegro*, including soft landings from jumps. They should have sufficient stretch in leg and upper back muscles for an easy flow of movement. All female professional ballet dancers are expected to dance on *pointe*, and that work is facilitated by a compact foot that arches easily and that has short toes, which are even in length.

All dancers would like to have smooth, straight legs, but in fact most people have legs that are knock-kneed, bowed, or hyperextended (swaybacked) to some degree. If these conditions are minimal, they, and other mild postural deviations, can be improved through practice of better body alignment and careful attention to the proper execution of ballet exercises.

Hyperextended knee—often accompanied by tilted pelvis, weight pushed back on the heel, and knee locked.

Knee brought into better alignment—often achieved by centering the pelvis, shifting the weight forward over the center of the foot, and developing muscular control to keep the knee stable

## BODY THERAPIES AND CONDITIONING METHODS

Deviations in body structure and restrictions in range of movement sometimes require more specialized exercises, including those that can change habitual movement patterns and strengthen or stretch the appropriate muscle groups necessary for certain actions. The dancer today has a number of body therapy and conditioning methods from which to choose for such specialized work. These methods not only can enhance the quality of movement, but they also can be effective means of rehabilitating the body after injury. Some of the more common body therapies are discussed briefly below. Because they involve re-educating and retraining the body, study should begin with a recognized expert in the particular method chosen.

## Ideokinesis

*Ideo* (for "thought") *kinesis* (for "motion") is the name given by Dr. Lulu E. Sweigard for her method of reeducating the body for more efficient movement and better balanced alignment. It involves mentally concentrating on visualizing a movement (such as a "perfectly" executed *grand battement*) without physically performing it. Specific images, based on a sound understanding of anatomy and biomechanics, are given by the teacher for particular movement patterns. The student concentrates on these while standing or simply lying in the Constructive Rest Position (CRP), a relaxing position requiring no muscle effort. In her work with dance students at the Juilliard School, Sweigard demonstrated that neuromuscular responses could be improved and changed by using correct mental images.

## Alexander Technique

Muscle relaxation and freeing of tensions in order to achieve more efficient movement patterns and body alignment also are integral to the Alexander Technique, developed by Frederick Matthais Alexander, an Australian actor. Central to his technique is the concept of "primary control," a term that refers to the correct use of the head and neck in relation to the entire body. "Forward and up" is the phrase used in thinking of the head balancing effortlessly on the spine.

In the Alexander Technique, analysis of inefficient movement patterns can lead to "inhibition" of those faulty habits through visualizing correct movements and by carefully practicing basic actions such as sitting, standing, and bending. This is done individually by a teacher giving verbal instructions and using a hands-on approach, communicating directly through touch to improve "the use of self."

Dancers using the Alexander Technique experience an ease in becoming placed up and over their legs and an improvement in coordination and in using their head, especially in spotting for turns.

CRP, the Constructive Rest Position, designed by Dr. Lulu E. Sweigard, can help relieve muscle strain and enhance relaxation. By using visualization techniques in this position, one can then begin to affect skeletal realignment.

## Bartenieff Fundamentals

The Bartenieff Fundamentals refer to a series of movement sequences aimed at developing more efficient movement patterns with particular attention given to movement quality. Integral to each movement sequence is finding how and where in the body the sequence should correctly begin. Proper initiation of a movement is crucial if correct neuromuscular action is to follow. The purpose and function of each movement sequence is clearly stated, along with instructions on how to perform the action as well as on what to avoid.

Developed by Irmgard Bartenieff, who trained in dance in Germany in the 1920s, the Fundamentals are important components of the Laban Movement Analysis system, created by Bartenieff's teacher, Rudolf von Laban. Laban/Bartenieff Institutes of Movement Studies, located in New York City, Seattle, and Baltimore, offer an intensive one-year course called the Certification Program in Laban Movement Studies.

Dancers find new insights into their own body alignment and movement patterns using the Fundamentals sequences, which are premised on the belief that posture is as individual as a signature: It reflects a person's internal feelings and thus the individual body's unique "accommodation" to space.

## Feldenkrais Awareness

Breaking out of habitual movement patterns by increasing the ability to feel and visualize movements is the goal of the body reeducation method developed by Moshe Feldenkrais, founding director of the Feldenkrais Institute in Tel Aviv, Israel, and currently taught by certified Feldenkrais instructors in the United States.

At the Tel Aviv Institute, some 1000 "lessons" are presented, each aiming at specific learning experiences, including the development of deep or organic breathing patterns. Twelve of these lessons are given by Feldenkrais in his book, *Awareness Through Movement*. Students are advised to do one lesson nightly before going to sleep, gradually increasing movement repetitions from ten to twenty-five times or more. In the lessons, attention is focused on the smallest possible movements, requiring the student to concentrate on minute signals from the body and thus increase body and movement awareness.

## Pilates Technique

Pilates Technique refers to the method of body conditioning and strength training developed by Joseph Pilates, a German boxer of the 1920s whose work originally consisted of conditioning exercises performed on a floor mat. He later designed a muscle-strengthening machine, the Universal Reformer, a sliding horizontal bed on which the exerciser pushes or pulls against the machine's bars or straps. Resistance from the machine's springs is used to stretch and strengthen the muscles. Muscle lengthening, rather than muscle bulk, is important, beginning with the Pilates method of abdominal work to strengthen the center of the body.

Many professional dance schools now are equipped with special strength-training rooms where dancers can work out with machines or free weights such as barbells and dumbbells. Longer, leaner appearing muscles, a better aligned and more flexible body, and less strain on the joints should be goals for body conditioning programs, as they also should be for ballet training.

## Aerobics

Aerobic training can improve a dancer's overall stamina by providing a varied progression of moderate exercise designed to give an adequate overload for the heart and vascular system. Types of endurance fitness training best for dancers include swimming, walking, and nonimpact aerobics. The duration and frequency of aerobic exercise should be carefully considered according to individual needs.

## Massage

A massage session can be a relaxing treat for a healthy dancer as well as a helpful treatment for an injured dancer. Types of massage vary from general, light techniques to localized, deep-frictioning work. Massage therapy may include exercises in breathing and in stretching and releasing.

Massage can help relieve soreness, stiffness, and muscle spasm, and it can aid in recovery from injury by helping to stimulate blood circulation. After the injury is healed, massage can help break down scar tissue.

Today, some professional ballet companies have a masseur on their staff, who even travels with the company on tour, in order to help the dancers meet the demands of an intensive performance schedule and to help them avoid injury.

## PREVENTING INJURY

Almost any form of physical activity, certainly one as demanding as ballet, raises the possibility of injury, and even a well-proportioned, well-conditioned body will suffer from strenuous movements or stretches if inadequately warmed up. The fundamental exercises at the *barre* have as one of their important functions, then, the systematic warming up of the body. When these exercises are neglected before a rehearsal or performance, or by a latecomer to class, then injury is invited. Moreover, each *barre* exercise has its specific purpose, as was seen in Chapter 2. Incorrect or minimal performance of any of those exercises can result in aches and pains, sometimes serious injury.

The correct execution of each exercise is the dancer's fundamental safeguard against injury. This includes alternating movements of extension and movements of release. For example, in a *battement tendu*, the foot is extended along the floor until the muscles of the arches are contracted and the toes pointed for the fully extended position. In this position, the ankle is stretched tight, and the calf muscles are contracted. In returning to the closed position, the toes relax, then the arches, as the ankle releases and the entire foot is placed on the floor.

Whenever possible the weight should be momentarily transferred to both feet in a closed position. If this brief relaxation is omitted, cramps may occur along the sides or arches of the feet; when the relaxation is systematically omitted, the muscles in the calf and thigh may cramp. Eventually, those muscles will become hard and bulky, lacking the essential elasticity for ballet.

The order of exercises at the *barre* can also prevent a muscle-bound look. Exercises are done to all directions; that is *grands battements* done to the front, which contract the quadracep muscles of the thigh, are countered by *grands battements* to the back, which stretch those muscles. *Relevés*, which tighten the calf muscles, are followed by *demi-pliés*, which relieve that tension.

In beginning ballet classes, teachers usually find it more appropriate to convey the desired outcome of a movement rather than to analyze the elaborate patterning of the groups of muscles involved. They demonstrate and give a general description for the correct execution of a movement or pose, believing that ballet

> . . . has its own technique of definite and exact movements. *If these movements are performed correctly, the correct muscles will work.* If the movement is not performed correctly, wrong muscles will come into play. . . . The dancer cannot begin by trying to find out which muscles to use. The right effort will eventually ensure right muscle work.[2]

More specific information can be provided and assimilated as students advance in their training. Many university-based dance programs include courses in kinesiology especially geared to understanding the how and why of human movement as it relates to dance. Kinesiology courses incorporate study of the structure of the body (anatomy) and the function of the body (physiology), as well as sometimes biomechanics (principles and laws of mechanics, usually using quantitative data, as applied to the function of human movement). The practical benefits of kinesiology include the improvement of movement efficiency and learning how to avoid injury.

## INJURIES AND AILMENTS

"If it hurts, it's good for you," is not good advice; pain may well be the body's warning to cease dance activity. Following is a brief discussion of some injuries and ailments that can occur to dance students.

### Cramp

A sudden muscle cramp during class should be a vivid reminder to warm up properly and to guard against the buildup of tensions during exercises (for instance, when possible, return the weight to both feet between movements that use one leg only). A cramp can be relieved by immediate gentle stretching of the cramped muscle, accompanied by massage. Soreness may result, but if the cramp is *fully* relieved before work is resumed, there will be no serious damage.

## Muscle Soreness

Sore muscles, a fairly common complaint from students who are not used to practicing ballet exercises regularly, can be a kind of "sweet pain," seldom long-lasting or in any way debilitating. The best remedy is to increase circulation by working the muscle lightly again as soon as possible. Prevention of soreness, or its often-accompanying stiffness, includes, besides sufficient warming up and gentle stretching, an adequate warming down — end-of-class *battements*, *pliés*, and *ports de bras* exercises (the dancer's equivalent of a race horse's walking routine following the race).

## Muscle Strain

Dancers often display a stoical pride in ignoring or minimizing nagging pains that should alert them to the possibility of a serious injury. One such injury, called a strain, is a tearing of muscles and, in severe cases, tendons as well, usually occurring anywhere from the hips down. The common causes can be structural weakness, previous injury or severe illness, overuse, or incorrect execution of an exercise (sometimes the very first exercise at *barre*, the *plié*). A strain produces stiffness and pain when the injured part is used. Swelling can occur too, but it can be minimized if the following procedures are observed:

1. Immediately apply pressure to the injured part by snugly wrapping it with a wet elastic ("Ace") bandage.
2. Apply ice compresses for twenty to thirty minutes to the injury and to an area well above and below it.
3. Elevate the injured part and allow the body to rest.

A guideline to use is to continue the above procedures for fifteen minutes, followed by forty-five minutes without the ice, for a twenty-four- to seventy-two-hour period. Irritation and tissue swelling can be relieved by anti-inflammatory medications such as ibuprofen. Moist heat can be applied after all possibility of swelling is gone, usually at least twenty-four hours later. Even a minor strain or "muscle pull" must be allowed time to heal; it cannot be "worked out."

## Ligament Sprain

A sprain is damage to ligaments of a joint, occurring most frequently in the ankle joint, but sometimes in hip or knee joints. A violent stretch or twist or fall can produce a sprain, but so also can incorrect knee-to-foot alignment during jumps or overly zealous attempts to turn out the feet beyond the range permitted by the hip joint. The injured joint will be very painful and sometimes impossible to use. To achieve a speedy recovery, swelling must be controlled as quickly as possible. Immediate treatment should include the three procedures listed above: pressure, ice, and elevation (PIE, for short), then immobilization of the joint to avoid further tearing of ligament fibers. Any such taping or bandaging should be done by or in consultation with a specialist. Uninformed treatment can be injurious.

### Bone Dislocation and Fracture

The same preliminary treatment also applies to such other serious injuries as dislocations (a bone thrown out of joint) and fractures. Although it is relatively rare for a dancer to break a bone, it is relatively common for a dancer to have stress fractures. These tiny changes in a bone's structure usually occur in the feet or along the shin area and can be a result of dancing on a hard floor, overwork, inadequate rest, or faulty technique. Six weeks to two months of rest will heal stress fractures, but it is wise to consult a physician.

### Bruises

The most debilitating bruise for the dancer is the "stone bruise" on the ball of the foot, sometimes a result of repetitious jumping, especially on hard surfaces. Poorly executed exercises, such as *battements frappés* in which the foot is pounded against the floor during brushes outward, can contribute to a contusion or bruise. Cold compresses wrapped around the foot should be applied at once. Later, gentle stretching and application of moist heat may be helpful.

### Shin Splints

The most common definition given of shin splints is a minor tearing of the muscle attachments from the tibia (shinbone), resulting in soreness, pain, and swelling below the knee on the inner side of the front of the leg. Not only dancers, but anyone, can get shin splints if the arches of the feet are not being supported properly by the muscles and ligaments in the feet, thus resulting in pronation of the feet when bearing weight. Landing incorrectly from jumps (heels off the floor and/or without a *demi-plié*) and dancing on a hard floor can lead to shin splints.

Preventive tactics include careful pre-*barre* warm-ups that emphasize gentle stretching of the calf muscles and foot flexors. Two recommended exercises are the following:

Stretching exercises to help prevent shin splints

1. Press the heels to the floor and, keeping the legs and back straight, lean forward to take hold of a wall or the *barre*; remain in this position sixty seconds.
2. *Demi-pliés* and *relevés* performed with or without turnout.

Following class, a repetition of the first exercise is advised, plus the following stretch:

Stand on one leg and bend the other leg back at the knee, taking hold of that foot and keeping the knees near one another. Adequate space should remain between the heel and the buttock to protect the knee. Hold for sixty seconds; repeat with the other leg.

Pain from shin splints can be severe, and the usual treatments, though not always effective, are ice applications (to help reduce swelling) and then moist heat and rest. Occasionally, a half-inch thick sponge-rubber pad worn inside the heel of the shoe gives relief; arch supports or tape around the shins may be advisable in particular cases. Dancers subject to shin splints should consult a physiotherapist for specific exercises to help strengthen the muscles involved. If pain and local tenderness persist, they may signal a stress fracture.

## Tendinitis

Tendinitis is an inflammation of a tendon, its connective tissue, or its sheath, the latter normally secreting a protective lubricant. If this lubricant is defective, then pain may result after repeated motions involving a given tendon. Overwork of the connecting muscle or a severe blow to a tendon may cause tendinitis, or the cause may be idiopathic—that is, unknown. Unfortunately, the Achilles tendon, connecting the back of the heel and the calf muscles, is particularly vulnerable to inflammation, especially for dancers who have a shallow *demi-plié*. The first sign of tendinitis usually is a constricted, burning sensation that becomes more severe as the tendon cools following cessation of exercise. Swelling may accompany the pain, and the dancer will find it difficult to *relevé* or point the foot.

The most effective treatment is rest—a hard prescription for most dancers to follow—but if it is ignored, the tendon problem may continue much longer than necessary. Because the application of heat may provoke more pain, ice may be more satisfactory, but so also may contrast baths of hot and cold water in some cases. Certainly a physician should be consulted when pain and swelling are acute. Taping of the tendon by a specialist or heel lifts inserted in the shoes may be effective, along with rest.

## Knee Injuries

Persistent pain, redness, or swelling in the region of the knee are warning signs of a significant problem, perhaps a sprain or tear of the ligaments around the knee or a case of tendinitis. Other serious symptoms are a tendency for the knee to lock or to give way suddenly, or to be unable to straighten fully, any one of which may indicate a cartilage tear or the slipping of the patella. An orthopedic physician should be consulted for accurate diagnosis and treatment.

The student must constantly be aware of the possible hazards to knees if circular movements (*ronds de jambes*) and knee bends (*demi-* and *grands pliés*) are practiced incorrectly. A knee is strongest when straight, therefore *rond de jambe à terre* practiced incorrectly with a relaxed knee invites stress to the surrounding ligaments. Closing to a tight fifth position *demi-plié* and then straightening the knees in that position can result in twisting the knees, especially if true outward rotation is not occurring at the hip joint. "Sitting" in a *grand plié* or allowing the knees to fall inward when rising out of a *plié* also contribute to stresses on the knee joint.

## Back Ailments

Back pain most common to dancers is caused by muscle strain, accentuated by rotary or bending movements of the back. A female dancer may experience such strain in the lower back when incorrectly attempting a high *arabesque*, thus hollowing out the low, lumbar area rather than distributing the extension throughout the spine. A male dancer may find he has pain higher in the back as a result of lifting his partner when the lift was made off balance without his center of gravity over his feet or when fatigued. Muscle spasm in the back may be a signal of such hazardous activity.

For back pain associated with muscle spasm, warm whirlpools or baths can be effective because of the antigravity effect of the water. Application of ice massage and gradual stretching may give relief. If strain has occurred, rest is the best remedy, followed by carefully selected back exercises. For chronic back pain, hot pads, hot showers, and saunas can be helpful, but they are not curative.

A ruptured disc may also follow bending or lifting. Here the pain usually occurs quite low in the back and/or down the legs because the last two discs are the ones most commonly affected. Correct diagnosis between disc disease and muscle strain is sometimes difficult and requires considerable medical experience.

## Clicks, Snaps, and Pops

Painless clicks, snaps, or pops in the joints of the hips, knees, or ankles are often disturbing to students, who wonder whether they are doing something wrong. The answer, usually, is no; a click may merely indicate a bone rubbing against an unyielding tendon or ligament.

A snap or pop may be due to a thickened capsule around a joint; sometimes it may indicate the joint is poorly aligned. However, a painful click in the knee may signal cartilage damage. Any noisy joint that *hurts* should be checked by a physician.

## CARE OF THE FEET

No part of the body must meet as many demands from ballet as the foot, which is asked to assume positions and perform movements quite outside its usual range. Despite these unusual requirements, if a student assumes correct ballet positions and performs ballet movements correctly, the feet will be held in the proper anatomic position and will work as very effective levers. Remember that the correctly placed standing foot is evenly balanced on the tripod points of the heel, the base of the big toe, and the base of the little toe.

Ballet feet must be strong and flexible; therefore, a dancer's training must produce both strength and suppleness in the feet. The ideal foot for ballet training would have roundish toes, all of medium length; an ankle that moves freely, allowing the foot when flexed to form a right angle to the leg, and when pointed to form a straight line from toe to hip; and, for a beginning student, a medium arch (the highly arched, slender foot, although beautiful when pointed, may indicate weakness).

The foot is a complicated mechanism consisting of twenty-six bones held together by a system of ligaments forming arches (the inside and outside longitudinal and the transverse, or metatarsal), which are supported by muscles. Its inherent (and inherited) shape is extremely important, but it will change after years of ballet study. Because particular demands are made of the female foot in point work, the following prerequisites should be met before a student goes on point: (1) the completion of a minimum of two or three years of basic ballet training; (2) correct posture when standing *and* moving; (3) correct performance of all exercises on *demi-pointe* (supporting knee absolutely straight, feet free from any tendency to sickle in or out); (4) a minimum age of twelve.

The last requirement is as important for parents and teachers to consider as it is frustrating for aspiring ballerinas or overly ambitious parents to follow. The reason is clear, however; ossification (the process of bone formation) of the feet is not sufficient in most children under twelve to withstand the strain imposed on the still unsolidified bones by standing or dancing on the toes. Serious deformities or injuries may result.

## Daily Care of the Feet

Healthy feet must be clean. They should be thoroughly washed and carefully dried, especially between the toes. An absorbent foot powder should be used if the feet perspire. Tired feet can be revived by baths of contrasting temperatures—hot to cold to hot. . . . Long soaking should be avoided because it can cause cracks between the toes. Elevation of the feet can offer respite by reducing the amount of blood in the extremities.

## Foot Disorders

**Flat Feet**   The clinical flat foot is weak, has no arch, and will never serve a dancer. However, a flexible foot may appear to be flat when bearing weight but will show an arch when weight is removed. Such a foot must be disciplined not to "roll" when assuming ballet positions. This muscle conditioning sometimes produces discomfort along the inner border of the foot. It is not serious, but when it persists, a few days' rest is advised. When work is resumed, care must be taken that the student does not attempt to turn out beyond correct range. Special muscle-strengthening exercises may be recommended, including lots of *battements tendus* to develop the set of short muscles on the underside of the foot.

**Bunions**   A swelling at the first joint of the big toe, caused by inflammation and thickening of a bursa, is commonly called a bunion. The foot that has a tendency to bunion formation (often determined by looking at the feet of parents or siblings) will, in all probability, develop one in intensive ballet training, although careful training often ensures correct functioning of the foot in spite of its abnormal appearance. However, extreme care should be given to the selection of proper-fitting ballet shoes (see Chapter 1, "Clothing") and sensible, well-fitting street shoes. Moist heat applied before class and ice afterwards may alleviate some discomfort from an angered bunion.

## Minor Foot Ailments

Professional dancers assume great fortitude toward blisters, corns, and other occupational foot nuisances, which, of course, are encountered by many people who never danced a step in their lives (ill-fitting hose or street shoes can be a source of trouble for any pair of feet).

Dance students usually exist on a very limited budget, spending most of what extra money they have on ballet lessons and ballet shoes. Seeking professional treatment of foot problems is a luxury in which the student seldom indulges, unless and until a problem becomes acute. Some practical suggestions are offered for the prevention and treatment of minor disorders that may occur.

**Blisters**  Caused by excessive friction on a given area, blisters are best prevented by protecting the skin; that is, minimally, wearing ballet tights with feet (not ankle-length tights unless adequate socks are worn). Additional aids can be gauze pads, moleskin, or Band-Aids placed on the vulnerable site before the blister appears. Tender feet can be toughened by regular applications of tincture of benzoin and pampered by systematic use of talcum powder rubbed around the toes.

Sometimes a small blister need not be opened (thereby inviting the possibility of infection) but simply protected by a doughnut-shaped pad, the center of which can be filled with petroleum jelly. When a sizable blister occurs, the area should be cleansed with an antiseptic and the blister carefully drained—opened with a sterile needle that has been boiled or held in a flame—but without removal of the blister cap. The wound then should be painted with iodine and covered with a sterile gauze pad. Blisters that have been unroofed—that is, the overlying skin removed, thus exposing a tender area—heal more slowly. They must be carefully treated with an antiseptic and covered with a sterile pad to avoid the greater possibility of infection.

**Soft Corns**  Soft corns between the toes occur as a result of excessive pressure. Precautions include foam-rubber wedges or bunches of lamb's wool placed between the toes—but do not encircle them, as that might cut off the circulation.

**Hard Corns**  The prevention of hard corns is ultimately the elimination of the pressures that cause them (sometimes improper footwear). If the problem persists—and it often does for dancers on point—the least that the victim can do is to wear simple pads of moleskin, adhesive felt, or foam that are designed to disperse the pressure from the area. Horseshoe-shaped pads that do not cover the corn itself should be used in preference to circular (life buoy–shaped) ones, as the flesh eventually will work through the hole when the latter are used.

Corns on the ball of the foot can reflect a mechanical problem of the toe and/or metatarsal head and can be difficult to eliminate. A total understanding of the cause requires study by a professional podiatrist, who should also be the one to trim a corn.

**Callouses**  Callouses are usually protective devices—and very effective ones in the dancer's case. If the buildup of tissue becomes too great, simple abrasives can be used—callous file or pumice stone. Cracks or fissures can best be prevented by keeping the feet clean, by limiting the callous buildup, and by using a lubricant (petroleum jelly, baby oil, or the like).

**Toenail Problems**   Long toenails can cause trouble for dancers in soft ballet shoes, but most especially for dancers on point. Most dancers keep their nails cut much shorter than the average person does. Proper pedicure should conform to the contour of the toe, not to a line straight across, as toenail growth follows individual patterns. If, despite proper care, ingrown nails persist, they may be caused by improper shoes or possibly an inherited tendency. An operation that removes the nail plate and the deformed root portion is sometimes advised. Some relief can be obtained by soaking the foot for short periods several times a day in hot water and by placing a small amount of lamb's wool beneath the toenail edge.

Thickened nails can be caused by injury or fungous disease. They must be either thinned continually by the use of grinding devices or surgically removed (along with the root, which causes the problem). Dancers who do a great deal of point work often develop one or two thickened nails, which usually cure themselves by dropping off, revealing a new, normal nail underneath.

**Fungus**   No one cures fungus (the cause of athlete's foot, among other things), but it can be managed easily with fungicides. People apparently either have a tendency for fungus or not, and if they have and once become infected, then the potential is always present.

**Plantar Warts**   Plantar warts are caused by a virus and occur on the *planta*, or sole of the foot. The discomfort from a wart on a weight-bearing area of the foot can be a very real concern to a dancer. Surgical removal of plantar warts can keep dancers off their feet for many days, and, in severe cases, for weeks or months. If possible, have the warts treated chemically, a method frequently used by dermatologists, because dance activity can continue normally during such treatment.

## EATING HABITS

Dancers are concerned with the importance of creating a certain image on stage, where lights and costumes have the effect of adding pounds to the body. Dance students rightly conclude that steps of elevation and point work are much easier to perform and are less stressful to the anatomy when the body does not carry excess weight. But, in their zeal to stay thinner than would seem necessary by most ordinary standards, dancers and dance students sometimes ignore the fact that their bodies were designed for purposes other than dancing. The demands and expectations made of the dancer's body require necessary nutrients every day to produce good health, consistent energy, and a sense of well-being. In dealing with problems of overweight and fears of gaining weight, dancers must consider the quality of food as well as the quantity.

### Diet

Diet, to the dancer, should mean an habitual way of eating so that the body maintains itself with maximum energy and efficiency. If an overweight (or underweight) condition exists, it deserves the attention of a professional person who can prescribe a particular, corrective diet based on many things, including height, sex, age, metabolic rate, and bone structure.

No dancer or dance student should attempt a self-prescribed "crash" diet (which often leaves one tense, tired, and prone to illness and injury) or rely on tricky diet pills to control appetite artificially (weight thus lost often is regained as soon as the pills are stopped). Fad diets, although frequently the subject of dressing-room conversations ("I eat *nothing* but yogurt and celery"), are not the answer either because no single food contains anywhere near the fifty essential nutrients required for a healthy body.

## Eating Disorders

Eating disorders are serious issues of great complexity. Two types of eating disorders sometimes associated with a dancer's obsession with thinness are anorexia nervosa, a type of self-starvation, and bulimia, characterized by eating great quantities of food followed by laxative abuse and/or self-induced vomiting. A variety of causes are now recognized as possible contributing factors to these eating disorders — psychological problems, environmental pressures, as well as genetic and cultural background. Psychological therapy and, recently, drug therapy are used to treat these disorders. It is important to remember that

> [A]ny dancer suspected of having an eating disorder should be approached with concern and caution, with the understanding that you are dealing with a potentially volatile situation. . . . If you find you must confront someone because of a probable eating disorder, it is best to consult an eating disorders professional beforehand on how to approach the situation. Despite good intentions, confrontations can do more harm than good if handled improperly.[3]

Psychological counseling services at a university, medical clinic, or hospital can be consulted for advice.

## Proper Nutrition

A person subject to listlessness, frequent illness, and a generally low energy level may be suffering from poor nutrition. Just consuming a certain number of calories every day is no guarantee of good nutrition. Calories are the measure of energy released by the food a person eats, and the amount differs according to the kind of food. But any food should also provide a variety of substances — nutrients that are essential for the building, upkeep, and repair of tissues and for the efficient functioning of the body. According to their use, nutrients are classified as proteins (for body maintenance and growth), carbohydrates (for the most efficient energy fuel), fats (for some energy fuel and essential vitamins and fatty acids), and specific vitamins and minerals (for transformation of energy and regulation of metabolic functions).

Like other people who participate in active physical effort, dancers can observe a very direct connection between what is ingested into their bodies and their performing condition. Of particular importance is the maintaining and replenishing of body fluid.

> Drinking adequate fluid is essential for top performance. Body fluids have important jobs: fluid in the blood transports glucose to the working muscles and carries away lactic acid; urine eliminates waste products; sweat dissipates heat via the skin. If you lose too much sweat, and don't replace your fluids, you reduce your ability to provide adequate circulation to muscles, internal organs, and body surface. This not only hurts performance but can also endanger health.[4]

Besides water, fluid intake should include juices such as orange juice and lemonade. Remember that beverages containing alcohol (beer, wine) or caffeine (coffee, tea) cause increased urination and thus can have a dehydrating effect.

The minimum daily requirement of vitamins and minerals is sometimes a point of controversy. Many people, including many dancers, augment their daily menu with extra doses of vitamins, especially C and E, and with calcium supplements. It is thought that women may need additional iron in their diet because of the loss of blood during menstruation. But it should be remembered not only that these vitamins and minerals occur naturally in foods but that their supplements are no substitute for natural food. A well-balanced, nutritious diet is essential, and it may be totally adequate for the body's vitamin–mineral needs. Best results come from eating grains, beans, fish, and fresh fruits and vegetables.

Recent diet research places greater emphasis on the energy-producing qualities of carbohydrates than on the more traditional protein sources. Thus, a preperformance meal of pasta is more beneficial than one of steak. Dancers and dance students often are forced into unusual eating schedules. Ideally, their preclass or preperformance meal should be eaten three hours before the activity in order to allow time for digestion and absorption of food. Because this is not always possible, several light meals a day (eaten one to one and a half hours before the dance event) may have to be substituted for three normal meals.

## Food for Thought

Dancing doesn't demand a perfect body; you can dance well if you have "a feeling for movement and music, a sense of rhythm and good coordination."[5] As an adult, you are still growing; muscle size and bone strength increase as you exercise and will continue to do so. The image of the thin, frail-looking dancer of the 1960s and 1970s has changed; dancers now are larger, healthier, and more individual looking. Individual expression is important; the goal of dance training is the discovery and development of your individual quality and capacity for movement. As an adult, your age and experience, your sense of self and body awareness, can contribute to the mind–body adventure of beginning ballet study.

1. Celia Sparger, *Ballet Physique* (London: Adam & Charles Black, 1958), 10.

2. Celia Sparger, *Anatomy and Ballet* (London: Adam & Charles Black, 1982), 10.

3. Robin D. Chmelar and Sally S. Fitt, *Diet, A Complete Guide to Nutrition and Weight Control* (Princeton, N.J.: Princeton Book, 1990), 111.

4. Nancy Clark, "Nutrition. Fluids, Dehydration and Thirst Quenchers," *Dance Teacher Now* (September 1991), 19.

5. Ellen Jacob, *Dancing, A Guide for the Dancer You Can Be* (Reading, Mass.: Addison-Wesley, 1981), 39.

# CHAPTER 6
# THE BALLET PROFESSION

The college freshman who begins the study of ballet must realize that at a comparable age most dancers who aspire to a professional ballet performing career are already accomplished technicians, having had seven or eight years of training, and many are already employed by a professional company. Adults who begin ballet training in their early thirties must understand that many professional dancers consider retiring from the stage by age forty. What sort of life do these artists live, whose careers begin and end so early?

The present chapter offers a glimpse of the professional dancer in training and at work, and it gives the parents of would-be dancers some idea how to start children in ballet. Also discussed are some areas of the theater that the late-starting dancer may encounter as a member of a civic, a regional, or even a semiprofessional dance company. Mention is made of other ballet-related careers, many that are new since the "dance boom" of recent decades.

## THE YOUNG DANCER

The child who develops an interest in serious ballet study has very likely already enjoyed classes in some sort of creative dance or pre-ballet. By age ten, the physique, mind, and emotions are considered grown up enough to begin ballet lessons, and the child will start going to class twice a week, probably one afternoon and a Saturday morning. As classes become more frequent, they invariably will get in the way of exciting social or school-sponsored events. The dedicated youngster learns early that painful, unpopular sacrifices will have to be made in order to attend daily dance classes, a requirement in later stages of training. Ballet's emphasis on the body's capacity for a large range of movement requires training at an early age when greater lengthening and limbering of the muscles can occur, a training, moreover, not provided by sports activities.

Difficult decisions face both young students and their parents, partly because there is no assurance how far a child's talent will develop, how long a child's interest will last, or whether — after all the work, sweat, tears, money, and sacrifices — any concrete reward (a contract with a ballet company) will be forthcoming. The uncertainty of ending up with a dance job after years of training and, for a boy at least, the nagging reality that probably greater pay, prestige, and security could be achieved in almost any other field (plus the lingering, nineteenth-century notion that ballet is essentially a feminine art) are so persuasive to American parents that they seldom let a son begin ballet lessons, much less encourage him to prepare for a career as a dancer. Therefore, American boys have tended to begin ballet study at a later age than girls, and at a time when they are less dependent on their parents.[1]

Although a few schools offer both dance training and an accredited pre-college academic curriculum, serious ballet students who live anywhere but in a few large cities usually must prepare as best they can. Fortunately, many excellent teachers and schools can be found throughout the country.

The quality of a school can be ascertained by getting an expert's opinion, by visiting the school — even untrained eyes often can tell something about the quality of a dance class — and by making inquiries about the teacher's own ballet background. Such information may be sought from or corroborated by someone in the dance profession, perhaps at a nearby college or university. Civic and regional companies often can suggest schools associated with their organizations, but even these can range from excellent to barely adequate. One concrete criterion is: When does the teacher allow a student to go on point? If there are six-year-olds tottering around in point shoes, then the school must be avoided (see Chapter 5, "Care of the Feet"). Even if point work is not started until age twelve, have there been at least two preceding years of careful work and do students look straight when on point? If they sag — lower back hollowed out, knees wobbly, ankles rolling in or out — then they are not ready, and thoughtful students will go elsewhere.

## PROFESSIONAL PREPARATION

As a rule, by age seventeen or eighteen (that is, immediately after high school graduation), students with career aspirations will enter a professional ballet school. The training there may not be any finer than at the hometown or neighborhood studio (and possibly not as good because of overcrowded conditions in some professional schools). However, students will benefit from having their talents appraised by people in the profession and from seeing themselves in close comparison with the products of the professional schools. By taking classes from a school associated with a company, students will know when company replacements are needed, when auditions are scheduled, and when the school faculty thinks they are ready to take the audition.

There are other routes. A student can write to a company to request an audition, or sometimes auditions can be arranged when a company visits a town while on tour. Members of a touring company may spot a talent in a local studio; some companies conduct regular summer workshops that can serve as showcases for aspiring performers. Some students may elect to enter a university that offers a major in ballet and performing opportunities in campus-based or local companies.

But the surest way into the more prestigious professional ballet companies has come to be through the professional school associated with a given company. Companies like to mold their dancers into a common style and groom their soloists for the many roles in the repertory. Therefore, they give preference to a talented eighteen-year-old who can be enrolled in their professional school, rather than to an equally talented twenty-two-year-old who has already finished training elsewhere. In many cases, such as the National Ballet of Canada or the New York City Ballet, a company can oversee the entire preparatory period, from beginning children's classes to preprofessional ones. Graduation performances often are exciting concerts that are reviewed by critics, with an invitation to join the resident company extended to some lucky graduates.

Because the performing years are short, the ballet business must be entered early. Twenty years is considered a reasonable period for peak performance, even though stars may continue to enchant audiences well beyond that limit, as in the cases of Margot Fonteyn, Galina Ulanova, Alicia Alonso, and Rudolf Nureyev. Even so, statistics have shown that most company dancers are under age thirty.[2]

A traditional gateway to membership in a company has been by audition. Any audition requires patience — patience to wait one's turn, trying to keep muscles warm and enthusiasm at a high pitch while others are being judged; patience to stand for interminable minutes in a line next to other eager bodies, all the while being critically surveyed and evaluated according to the immediate, undisclosed needs of the company; patience to wait for another audition or possible openings in the company later on, if a first audition is unsuccessful.

An audition requires a certain protocol. Mamas, teachers, friends should be left at home. Stage makeup should not be worn; an audition is not a performance. Applicants should be dressed neatly and simply, as for a ballet class. They should come to the audition fully warmed up, able to dance the first combinations as well as possible, for there may never be a chance for later ones. The applicant should do exactly what the choreographer asks without adding personal variations. Following precise instructions, and quickly, is a requisite for the professional theater. It is a good idea to be prepared to perform a short solo or variation.

Nervousness is to be expected. But a body that has been well trained will not be destroyed by butterflies in the stomach. The carriage of the arms, the shape of the legs, the flexibility of the spine, the arch of the foot will remain, even if accompanied by a tense face or wobbly balance. The judges are professionals, but they, too, once had to audition for a first time, and they can recognize talent and training beneath a nervous skin.

Unfortunately, talent, good training, a reasonably attractive face, and a well-proportioned body are not guarantees of success at an audition. The supply of dancers with those qualities usually is much greater than the availability of positions in professional ballet companies. (Troupes that offer year-round employment in the United States are still relatively rare—perhaps a dozen or so at any one time.) Dancers often attribute their success (or more usually their lack of success) to politics (whom one knows) and luck (being in the right place at the right time).

## JOINING A COMPANY

The dancer who is successful at an audition will enter a relatively small, intimate community. Most American ballet companies have fewer than 30 dancers, even though the "big two," American Ballet Theatre and New York City Ballet, have close to 100 on their rosters. A company is headed by an artistic director—usually a choreographer, perhaps the chief one of the troupe—who, in consultation with the business administration of the company, makes all final decisions—repertory, promotions, hiring, firing. There may be associate or assistant directors. There will be a ballet master or mistress whose duties include rehearsing ballets and giving classes to company dancers.

The new member of the company will begin a daily regimen that, by most ordinary work standards, is strangely cloistered and far removed from the "real" world. It begins each day with class, a period of hard physical work. Every dancer, no matter how experienced, must do daily *pliés*, *battements*, and *ronds de jambe*. It is a humbling experience, for without the taxing daily exercises, no dancer's body will retain the strength and precision necessary for ballet performance, nor will technique improve.

## BALLET REHEARSAL

The class systematically warms up the dancer's body for the rehearsal period, which often follows directly. A dancer may spend two to five hours daily in rehearsals (sometimes more, for which overtime compensation is generally paid), and these may be called with little prior warning; dancers regulate their lives by notices on the rehearsal bulletin board.

At a rehearsal for a new ballet, it is the choreographer who is in charge and who is given the power to cast and compose the ballet of his or her choice.

These decisions must, of course, meet with the approval of the company director, but choreographers are entrusted with a great deal of power. How does one compose a dance? Ask a choreographer and receive a very personal answer; one method may work for one and quite another method for the next. Even the same choreographer may use different strategies with different ballets or dancers. The music for the ballet or the idea of the ballet may have whirred around in the choreographer's head for weeks, months, or years, but a first rehearsal sometimes produces only the most tenuous promise of what will develop. Some choreographers arrive at a rehearsal with notepads full of explicit details for gestures, movements, and floor patterns; others prefer to experiment there, letting chance happenings or even accidents suggest movement possibilities. All must respond to the particular qualities of the dancers assembled for their ballet. Even if the choreographic process appears random, it usually is following the broad, basic structure of the dance because it has been viewed time and time again in the mind of the choreographer.

Almost without exception, choreographers for professional ballet companies are former dancers themselves, and most of them therefore learned the craft of choreography by apprenticeship, watching a master choreographer at work while they participated as dancers in the creation of a new ballet. This background enables choreographers to draw upon a large movement vocabulary, which they then are able to demonstrate. One choreographer may expect the cast to imitate movements exactly; another may merely indicate the desired movement in the barest outline, preferring to see how the dancers themselves continue and fulfill the movement. A rehearsal can be an exciting creative experience for all concerned.

Once the details are worked out for each dance sequence, they are practiced over and over again. Some choreographers never change a single step once it has been set, but others redo, throw out, start again. During rehearsals for a new ballet, a dancer learns to keep several versions of one sequence in memory—a prodigious task because the same dancer will have roles to remember, rehearse, and perform in many other ballets. Beginning students are wise to cultivate dance "memory" as they are learning dance technique: Try to reconstruct an entire class by memory. Practice doing this every day while the experience of dancing is still fresh. Eventually a dancer's muscles provide a memory storehouse; they seem to respond without conscious mental effort.

Human memory and word of mouth have been the links between the choreography of one generation and the dancers of the next, although today more and more use is being made of videotape and dance notation. (See "Recording Dance," discussed later in this chapter.) A skilled dance notator is a valuable asset for the preservation of a company repertory and the establishment of a choreographic library. But, the rare dancer (and there are a few) whose memory can recall every step of every dancer in a given ballet is still a most treasured member of the fleeting world of ballet.

Another valuable member of any ballet company is the rehearsal pianist, who may sit for hours replaying the same short passage of music until a choreographic problem has been solved and the sequence learned by the dancers. When a reliable pianist is not available, a choreographer may rehearse with a tape recorder. Or, if music is being composed especially for the ballet, the dancers may hear only counts at rehearsal. Because of ever-increasing production and rehearsal costs, a complete orchestral score may not be heard before the first stage rehearsal.

In all cases, counting of the musical bars or phrases is done in great detail by dancers and choreographers alike; very, very seldom is any movement improvised on the ballet stage. Even large crowd scenes in some of the classical ballets are planned down to minute details of who goes where and when and how. Stage rehearsals are tedious but necessary parts of the dancer's life. Before the initial performance of any ballet, it must be seen on stage, costumes must be danced in, lighting plans must be tried, and the orchestra must be rehearsed with the dancers.

Companies that tour extensively learn to adapt to all kinds of theater conditions. They are likely to find a differently proportioned stage at every stop—wide and shallow, narrow and deep, square, semicircular—and theaters with skimpy wings making leaping exits hazardous at best. New stages call for adjustments and sometimes particular movements will need to be modified or changed but these revisions are worked out before performance, not during it.

A dancer's sense of space becomes finely tuned. Relationships to other dancers must be kept, and distances from the sides or front or back of the stage must be preserved. This is not accomplished with a yardstick or the counting of floorboards, although visual aids can include such visible features as an auditorium's lighted exit signs, aisles, or openings into the wings. But through training during rehearsals, dancers learn to relate quickly to distances and to remember spatial patterns.

Occasionally, a company on tour will arrive at a new theater with insufficient time to rehearse the evening's performance fully. The best they can do is to "block" the dances on the new stage, the dancers walking through their parts and, by means of a kind of elaborate hand and finger sign language, indicating the steps that later will be performed in those spots.

## BALLET PERFORMANCE

Backstage, the stage manager or *regisseur* tries to oversee the preperformance activity that, to a visitor, may resemble chaos. Stagehands lug equipment, scenery, and props. Lighting technicians preside over a maze of wires and towers (light "trees"). Wardrobe ladies, mouths full of pins, may be making last-minute alterations. Each person does his or her specific job; union regulations forbid the overlapping of backstage tasks. Amid the dust and drafts and commotion, the dancers, bundled in layers of wool, go through *barre* exercises, holding onto any wall or chair or ladder available.

Where is the magic that will soon be seen on stage? It is slowly forming in the minds and muscles of the dancers. The ritual of warming up is one of several that prepare the dancers for performance and preoccupy the nerves. Makeup is another. Dancers cover their everyday faces with carefully applied stage makeup more elaborate than that used by other stage artists because it must stand up under the rigors of fast movement, varied lighting, and profuse perspiration.

For women there is another ritual—that of preparing point shoes. Each dancer personally sews on the ribbons of her shoes and breaks in each pair according to her own method—ranging from simply walking around in the shoes, to soaking them in water, to slamming a door on them (when off the feet, of course!). The "box" of the shoe is in reality only several layers of cloth held together by a strong glue. The rest of the support comes from a leather sole and shank. Point shoes break in easily, and their life is short. A ballerina may use a new pair of shoes for each act of a ballet; a member of the *corps de ballet* may have to make do with only one new pair a week. Fortunately, shoes are provided by the company, and they are handmade by skilled craftsmen who build each pair of shoes according to a mold of each individual dancer's foot.

As curtain time approaches, the dancers help zip or hook each other into their costumes. Hairdos are given a final layer of spray. Toe shoe ribbons are checked for the twentieth time (a loose ribbon is a dancer's nightmare). *Demi-pliés* and *battements tendus* keep pace with the flutter in the stomach. Nervousness can attack the dance novice and dance veteran alike, but most, probably all, pride themselves on being troupers. They know that their nerves are bringing their bodies to the high pitch necessary for performance.

## LOOKING AT THE BALLET

What does the audience see as the curtain opens? The merely interested but ballet-uneducated public will immediately see movement with a capital M, for that is the prime of ballet. They will see living sculpture created by a lifted leg and an outstretched arm—and the spaces framed by those limbs that become important designs in themselves. Members of an audience may not know whether a movement is done correctly, but they can sense its quality. Fellow humans are dancing, often expressing human feelings in dramatic situations, and the emotions and muscles of the audience have an empathic response. Costumes and stage designs help set the appropriate scene; lighting underscores the appropriate mood. Above all, the music is linked to the spectacle on the stage. Some, or all, of these elements are employed—even in a so-called abstract ballet—to carry the audience along a choreographer's intended path.

Among the members of the audience are the dance critics, who usually have the advantage of having seen a great many ballet performances, thereby gaining some yardstick with which to assess one ballet evening or one ballet trend with another. They know that the repertory of most companies typically represents three or four types of ballets: revivals of or excerpts from nineteenth-century European or Russian story-ballets (such as *Giselle* or *Swan Lake*); early twentieth-century one-act ballets from various Ballets Russes companies (such as *Les Sylphides* or *Gaité Parisienne*); works by leading choreographers of the mid-twentieth century (such as *Serenade* or *Theme and Variations* by George Balanchine); and contemporary ballets that may have been composed by the director of a given company. An acquaintance with ballet history is essential for an informed opinion from a critic or a patron of the ballet (see Chapter 7).

Reviewing the New York dance scene, critic Marcia B. Siegel observes:

> Seeing is a very selective, individual and concrete process, and it means more to me than opinion. . . . Each separate dance experience carries its own unique and momentary life, but to consider *only* that singular evening's lifetime, it seems to me, is to deny evolution, to deny civilization.[3]

A dancer can inevitably and almost instantly sense an audience's approval or disapproval, its involvement or its boredom. Audience reactions can change during the course of an evening, and it is the performer's particular pleasure to change indifference to enthusiasm. An audience's support, with appropriate laughter or hushness, is intoxicating to the performer, who may receive the final tribute of applause in a state of outward calm but inward jubilation.

## AFTER THE SHOW

Coming down from the high emotional pitch of a performance is not easy. A dancer may long to repeat the whole show immediately. The body is warm and loose, the nerves are calm, the unknown has been faced and conquered. Now, one could really perform! No thrill, physical or spiritual, could compare with those moments of power onstage — pity the person who is not a dancer!

Backstage, chatter is almost exclusively about the performance that has just ended. The dancers, unwilling to let go of the magic they have created, must nevertheless get back to reality. Costumes must be hung, faces must be cleansed of all makeup, bags must be packed. The dancer's body, which has just spent several hours fluctuating between near exhaustion and instant recovery, cries out for food and fluids. The company heads for a late-night restaurant or to a reception that a local organization may have prepared in their honor. Deprived of stage makeup and colored lights, the dancers look appallingly pale and much smaller than they did on stage. But these people are athletes, even though they are trained to conceal all effort, and when the night's work is finished, they need to replenish their bodies with an ample meal.

Dancers realize that they live in a separate world. They grew up in ballet classrooms; they were socialized in studio dressing rooms and rehearsal halls. As professionals, their six-day-a-week schedule permits them little time for interests or friends outside the dance profession; it even permits them little sunshine. They are like hardy indoor houseplants who thrive under artificial lights—of the theater.

Reflecting on the dancer's commitment, Robert Weiss, a principal dancer with New York City Ballet, said:

> It's a very funny profession. . . . You get into it at such a young age. . . . It's not only a profession, it's a way of life. . . . Despite all the problems, mental and physical, the company politics and all that stuff, there's a reward in dancing that's indescribable. It's just different from any of the other performing arts—the mental and physical coming together. And when everything is right—two or three times a year, maybe— well . . . there's no other feeling like it and you remember that and you'll do almost anything to feel that again.[4]

Onstage, dancers are magicians; offstage, they tend to be supremely disciplined, practical, punctual people. The "fairy princess and prince charming" leave the theater, returning home (or back to hotel rooms) to do the inevitable evening laundry of sweaty leotards and tights. They look forward to such simple luxuries as a hot bath and a night's sleep as few others can appreciate. Is this a "real" life? What of the future? Next year or the next? The tired dancers focus on tomorrow. There is class to take at ten-thirty in the morning.

## NONPROFESSIONAL CIVIC AND REGIONAL COMPANIES

The traditional route to the professional ballet stage just described is not realistic for the adult beginner, but performing opportunities sometimes exist in nonprofessional companies throughout the United States. Certain repertories may call for more mature dancers who may not necessarily need advanced levels of technique.

Serious amateur dancers have benefited from the establishment of civic ballet companies, a movement begun in 1941 by Dorothy Alexander in Atlanta. Gradually, local ballet companies began to work together to sponsor performances and dance festivals. In 1963 the National Association for Regional Ballet (NARB) was established, also with inspiration from Alexander, to promote high performing and teaching standards through mutual communication, sharing of membership resources, and annual regional performance festivals. A few regional companies eventually attained professional status, paying company members the federal minimum wage for a minimum of thirty weeks a year and maintaining an annual budget of a certain amount. One such company is the Atlanta Ballet.

## OTHER BALLET-RELATED CAREERS

The increasing popularity of dance in general, since the "dance boom" of the 1970s and 1980s, has created the need for knowledgeable experts in numerous ballet-related fields, now located in many parts of the country besides the large dance centers of the east and west coasts.

## Teaching and Choreography

Teaching and choreographing are two traditional nonperforming careers that immediately come to mind. Both require an intensive dance background, but not necessarily a professional performing one. University and college dance curricula vary, but most offer courses in choreography ("composition classes"), creative movement for children, and teacher training ("methods classes"). The latter usually is geared toward public school teaching (dance has enjoyed a significant increase in elementary and secondary schools) and college programs (where a master's degree is routinely expected for a faculty appointment, especially in lieu of professional dance experience).

Career preparation for private studio teaching has been haphazard in the United States, where no certification or licensing requirements obtain. Yet the challenges of running a commercial studio call for a careful program of study:

> Whether offered by a university, a conservatory or a professional studio, such a program should require studies in a variety of dance techniques with special emphasis on teaching beginners and preschool creative movement. It should require instruction in preparing course outlines spanning a greater number of development years than most public school or university teachers face when dealing with the progress of a single student. Curriculum planning would need to identify long-range goals as well as detail the construction of daily, monthly and yearly class plans which allow for physically sound and emotionally satisfying progression in technique and also some initial experience in composition for the student. Selection of accompaniment, improvisation, creating combinations and studies for different levels to achieve specific technique goals, educational theory and instructional methods, child development, psychology, anatomy or physiology, choreography, production, studio organization, administration, promotion, business practices and financial management should all be a part of the studio teacher's preparation. A little advice on dealing with stage mothers and some basic professional ethics would not be amiss.[5]

## Recording Dance

Recording dance, either by special notation or by videotape and film, is an expanding field that offers great benefits to both the dance world and the community at large. Its purposes are

> to preserve masterworks for future generations; to increase the availability of the work beyond its immediate performance; to provide accurate tools for stylistic and structural analysis by the historian, critic, and researcher . . .; to furnish students and choreographers with material for study. Anthropologists, ethnologists, and sociologists look at recorded movement for clues to the work habits and folk dances of other cultures.[6]

Skilled technicians, sensitive to the special requirements of the dance, are needed for preserving dance on film or videotape, as well as for compiling cassettes or filmstrips for instructional use. The popularity of dance on television and in movies creates a demand for better production by those industries.

As a method of recording dance, however, film or tape usually must be augmented by notation. Many methods have been tried and used since the fifteenth century. Today, the two notation systems most used are Labanotation (developed by Rudolf Laban and first published in 1928) and the Benesh method, also known as Choreology (developed in England in the 1950s).

An increasing number of college dance programs offer courses in notation. Special training programs frequently are offered by the Dance Notation Bureau in New York City, which also secures work for many notators (those who write down movement in a notation system) and reconstructors (those who restage a notated dance). The use of computerized equipment makes this an exciting, innovative field.

## History, Research, and Criticism

Reconstruction of dances from older types of notation has given recent impetus to the field of dance history, an endeavor that combines research, writing, and performance with knowledge of music, art, theater, social customs, and dance. Thus, the Renaissance or Baroque dance scholar is in demand by early music festivals, art museums, libraries, theater companies, and college dance, music, and drama departments. A specialist in nineteenth-century social dance, such as dance-historian Elizabeth Aldrich, often is hired to stage dance scenes in period films.

Ballet companies interested in reviving long-lost works have employed dance researchers and reconstructors to restore important dances to today's stages. For example, the Joffrey Ballet has added to its repertory the 1847 *pas de six* from *La Vivandière*, choreographed (after Antonio Guerra) by Arthur Saint-Léon and reconstructed by Ann Hutchinson Guest from Saint-Léon's own notation system. Such activity has helped establish respect for dance scholarship within the profession.

Educational academies have encouraged reconstruction projects, such as the 1991 performance at the Juilliard School of Vaslav Nijinsky's 1912 ballet, *L'Après-Midi d'un Faune*. Students were given Labanotation transcriptions of Nijinsky's own notated score, from which they read their own part in preparation for rehearsals.

Training of dance writers, researchers, and critics is beginning to be found on more college campuses. The establishment in 1982 of the first United States graduate program in dance history (at the Riverside campus of the University of California) is but one example. Certain dance courses (especially dance history) are accepted as arts and humanities options in general college requirements.

Newspapers and periodicals are featuring more dance articles, thus employing more writers and critics whose specialty is dance. In the United States, the Congress on Research in Dance, the Dance Critics Association, and the Society of Dance History Scholars help promote dance as an area for research, as do similar organizations in Great Britain and continental Europe.

Dance scholars must have access to libraries. Of particular value are the dance holdings at the Harvard Theatre Collection, the San Francisco Performing Arts Library and Museum, and the Library of Congress in Washington, D.C. Most impressive of all is the Dance Collection of the New York Public Library, located in the Performing Arts Research Center at Lincoln Center in New York City. It contains over 30,000 books on dance, 600 periodical subscriptions, 355,000 dance manuscripts, and 10,850 dance videotapes and films. In addition, it has collections of ballet libretti, pictures and prints, original drawings and designs, ballet programs and newspaper clippings, and 4600 hours of oral history audiotapes. The multivolume catalog of the Dance Collection now is available on CD ROM, entitled "Dance on Disc."

## Therapy and Medicine

Among areas of growth in the field of dance-related activities are dance therapy and dance medicine, little-known professions prior to the 1940s even though dance and healing have been associated since ancient times. The American Dance Therapy Association defines dance therapy as "the psychotherapeutic use of movement as a process which furthers the emotional and physical integration of the individual."[7] Those who may benefit are

> individuals who require special services because of behavioral, learning, perceptual and/or physical disorders; and rehabilitation of emotionally disturbed, physically handicapped, neurologically impaired and the socially deprived of all ages, in groups and individually.[8]

Both graduate and undergraduate degree programs in dance therapy allow academic specialization in this field, with workshops and special courses offering additional preparation.

Dance medicine, focusing on the special needs of dancers, has begun to attract physicians, some of whom are hired by professional dance companies. Through scientific research, testing, and publication, the field of dance medicine has increased our understanding of basic ballet principles — for example, the order and repetition of *barre* exercises.

## Administration and Management

Arts administration and management are areas of increasing need and diversity as companies, festivals, and programs seek funding and bookings, coordinate arts events and publicity, and deal with legal and budgetary matters. Training programs in arts management and administration include workshops as well as degree programs at universities, but many posts, because of their varied requirements, require on-the-job training.[9]

## Production

Obvious performance-related fields include such vital areas as stage and theater design, costuming and lighting, and music accompanying, composition, arranging, and conducting. The skilled technical director or stage manager, who can oversee these diverse aspects of production, is highly prized.

## Volunteer Assistance

Every dance organization benefits from well-informed, dance-loving people who may serve on boards of directors of companies, on the guilds of schools, or in a host of other service capacities connected with ballet production and education. The energy, ideas, and enthusiasm of such people provide invaluable assistance to the entire field of dance. Not the least important in this category are the informed, sympathetic members of the audience who regularly attend and support dance concerts. All these "volunteers" deserve a sincere bow of gratitude from the dance community.

As this brief discussion illustrates, there is more to the dance field than dance. But, no matter what ballet-related vocation (or avocation) is pursued, it is pursued best by persons who have had some dance training. So the first rule of preparation for any of these careers is: Buy some basic dance equipment (see Chapter 1, "Clothing"), enroll in the best school available, and study ballet technique diligently (and perhaps other dance techniques as well). Make a habit of attending dance performances. When possible, join local or campus performing groups and participate (onstage or backstage) in theater productions. Observe master teachers conducting technique, composition, or improvisation classes. Observe choreographers conducting rehearsals. These years of preparation can occur along with other training or other jobs because such dance classes, rehearsals, and performances frequently take place in the evening or on weekends. Even when dreams of being a professional dancer are not the goal, one can pleasurably (and perhaps even profitably) take part in the world of ballet. Class just may begin at seven-thirty in the evening!

## NOTES

1. Ronald Federico, "Recruitment, Training, and Performance: The Case for Ballet," in Phyllis Stewart and Muriel Cantor, eds. *Varieties of Work* (Boston: Schenkman, 1973). Federico's research is based on interviews with approximately one-half of all dancers in 1968 who were members of professional ballet companies in the United States. He reports that only 11 percent of his male respondents claimed to have been influenced toward dance training by their families, while 54

percent of women made this claim. Correlatively, 86 percent of the females had begun ballet lessons by age eleven in contrast to only 22 percent of the males.

2. Federico, *ibid.*, reports that only 11 percent of his interviewees were under nineteen years of age and only 13 percent were over twenty-nine, which suggests that fully three-quarters of all professional dance company members in the United States are in the age range of nineteen to twenty-nine.

3. Marcia B. Siegel, *Watching the Dance Go By* (Boston: Houghton Mifflin, 1977), xvi.

4. Quoted in *The Los Angeles Times*, 11 June 1981.

5. Mimi Marr, "Where Do They Go When the Dancing Stops?" *Dance Magazine* (September 1975), 64.

6. Linda Grandey and Nancy Reynolds, "Recording the Dance," *The Dance Catalogue*, ed. Nancy Reynolds (New York: Harmony Books, 1979), 194.

7. Kayla Kazahn Zalk, "Dance Therapy: The Oldest Form of Healing and a New Profession," *The Dance Catalogue*, ed. Nancy Reynolds (New York: Harmony Books, 1979), 205.

8. *Ibid.*

9. An example of the complex, specialized nature of running a large ballet company is revealed in the following news item about a 1992 tour by American Ballet Theatre: "For a touring company as large as ABT, however, with its 76 dancers and 45 traveling staff members, there's no way to leave New York City without first purchasing 1,500 airplane tickets and bringing along six portable computer terminals, 5,000 pairs of shoes, 900 to 1,000 costumes, 300 wigs, $5,000 in cosmetics, a washer and dryer, to say nothing of 50 gallons of liquid detergent and 40 gallons of fabric softener." (*San Francisco Chronicle*, 17 January 1992.)

# CHAPTER 7
# BALLET HISTORY

One of the intriguing questions dance enthusiasts today would like to ask dancers of the past is, How exactly did you dance? Correlatively, ballet dancers of today may well wonder about the origins and evolution of the dance technique and style they are expected to master in today's classrooms and to perform in contemporary theaters.

Accounting for the past is not an easy task in the dance realm. Of all the arts, the art of movement is the most ephemeral—disappearing almost as it occurs, leaving few and inexact records of its brief glory. ("Ballet is now . . . now is when it happens" was a familiar saying of choreographer George Balanchine, founder and artistic director of the New York City Ballet until his death in 1983.)

In this century, technological developments in film and videotape allow a certain preservation of today's repertories that dances of earlier centuries never enjoyed. Recent respect for, but by no means universal use of, newly improved dance notation systems encourages relatively accurate preservation of contemporary choreography. (See Chapter 6, "Recording Dance."). But much of ballet's history, especially its technical and choreographic history, has been lost for lack of a generally accepted and precise recording device. Unlike students of opera, drama, or painting—who can study and practice from scores, scripts, or canvases—dance students have to rely almost exclusively on personal contact with practitioners of their art. Exactly what did the dancing masters of the past teach their pupils? Seeking that answer has become the focus of much recent research in dance history and will be the theme of this brief survey.

## A TRADITION BEGINS

To trace the tradition of instruction from dancing master to pupil inherited by today's ballet instructors and students, one can begin in the fifteenth century with the appearance of a new aid for an old art—a dance instruction book. Sometime around the 1440s, a professional dancing master wrote down what to dance and how to dance it, thus allowing later generations to re-create, with substantial understanding, technique and choreography now over 550 years old. Like manuals by subsequent authors, this treatise, *De arte saltandi e choreas ducendii* ("Of the art of leading *saltandi* and *choreas*")[1] by Domenico da [from] Piacenza, did not forecast the future but described the inherited dance tradition of its own time. Thus, it is possible that Domenico's dances represent an even earlier tradition, and it is certain that they did not expect to be connected to a then-unknown genre, classical ballet. Nonetheless, historian Ingrid Brainard points out that Domenico's choreographies include two miniature dance dramas, perhaps "the first two real ballets."[2]

## BACKGROUND TO THE TRADITION

Without instruction books, a discussion of dance prior to the fifteenth century can be only speculation, advised by careful study of dance artifacts. These artifacts include evidence from musical scores, literary references, artistic depictions, clerical diatribes against dancing, philosophical advocacy for dancing, and a host of other secondary sources.

We know, for instance, from cave drawings that ancient peoples, sometimes costumed as animals, employed dance in a variety of ways. Judging by tribal dances today, movements were well organized and could be rhythmically complex, humorous as well as serious.

Egyptian tomb paintings depict solemn religious dancing of funeral processions patterned on the legend of the devoted Isis mourning for her beloved husband–brother, the god Osiris. Also portrayed are exuberant, acrobatic secular entertainments associated with those rites.

This dual nature of dance–ennobling and intoxicating—was evident in Greek culture also, as Plato noted: "Movement of the body may be called dancing, and includes two kinds; one of the nobler figures, imitating the honorable, the other of the more ignoble figures, imitating the mean."[3]

Whether associated with gestures of the noble chorus in the great dramatic tragedies or the rowdy, satirical dances of comedies and satyr plays, Greek dancing cannot be reconstructed with any certainty—this despite the many visual sources, such as sculpture and vase decoration, documenting the integral place of dance in Greek life as private entertainment, communal activity, or religious ritual. Western theatrical dance has reflected, from the sixteenth century onward, Greek influence in thematic material and in costuming. Western education in the nineteenth and twentieth centuries has championed the benefits of dance to health and harmonious physical development, as did the ancient Greeks. The choice of *orchesis* (Greek for "dance") as the name of college dance clubs underscores that connection.[4]

Greek theaters (*theatron*, "place for seeing") have had their influence as well. They were outdoor amphitheaters, rising along a concave slope of a hill in a three-quarter circle of seats above a level, circular performance area called an *orchestra*. Behind that circular area, and opposite the spectators, was the *skene*, a structure whose facade provided a background, perhaps a temple, for the play, and whose interior served as a dressing area for the performers. Principal characters appeared from a central doorway, and entrances on either side provided other access.

As the Romans began conquering the surrounding countryside, they copied or adapted aspects of Greek drama and theater, resulting in a gradual decline in the close relationship that dance had enjoyed with song, verse, and dramatic expression in the earlier hellenistic period. For an empire of peoples sharing no common language, for audiences who preferred exciting and colorful spectacles to classic dramatic forms, Roman theatrical fare developed danced interpretations emphasizing movement and gesture rather than verse and song. Highly skilled pantomime artists (*panto*, "all"; *mime*, "acting out") such as Pylades, a specialist in the tragic style, and Bathyllus, a comic virtuoso, enjoyed great wealth and considerable political power. The acrobatic nature of some of the *pantomimi* can be appreciated from written accounts at the time:

> He [the dancer] leaps on one foot then on both, stands on his right foot, and lifts his left leg up to his breast and shoulder, bends it round his back to his neck, whirls around, bent over backwards, so fast that his head seems to circle on the ground.[5]

Roman outdoor theaters were huge and opulent. The stage, raised about 5 feet high, could be as much as 300 feet long and 40 feet deep. The simple *skene* of Greek theaters became highly decorated facades whose columns and statuary could dwarf the performers. The orchestra area was reduced to a semicircle, used less for dancing than for seating important spectators or, on occasion, even flooded for performance of water spectacles.

A preference for spectacle over content saw the great pantomime artists gradually replaced by *mimi* specializing in lewd farces. These increasingly lascivious popular entertainments, along with circus games and gladiatorial combats, were denounced by the Christian Church in Rome. Eventually, as Christian emperors replaced pagan ones and as the Church grew in power, dance in its various forms was, essentially, forbidden and the entertainers dispersed.

## DANCE IN THE MIDDLE AGES

Even as the Church fathers preached against dancing as a form of bodily pleasure that impeded preparation for the spiritual afterlife, Christian theologians frequently employed dance imagery to extol the harmony of the universe and of the soul with that universe: "The whole cosmos takes part in the dance. Whosoever does not take part in the dance does not know what shall come."[6]

The period from the fifth to the fourteenth century (from the decline of the Roman Empire to the beginning of the Renaissance), known as the Middle Ages, was not devoid of earthly dance. A variety of entertainers—jugglers, acrobats, conjurers, minstrels, and dancers—were familiar to medieval fairs, marketplaces, and village greens. Of these, the minstrel, who sang and played an instrument, was a kind of voice for society in the absence of theaters and before the invention of the printing press. He could pass along the great legends, epic poems, and ballads of humanity as well as satirize the established order— clergy, aristocrats, and peasants.

In France, in 1330, journeymen jugglers and minstrels decided to form their own guild, following the example of other trades and in recognition of their increasing popularity as entertainers for an aristocracy growing in wealth and worldliness.[7] Certain changes in medieval life had begun in the eleventh century as the hold of the Church loosened. The rise of the towns, establishment of universities, development of large-scale commerce, and exchange with other cultures during the Crusades all contributed to the flowering of European civilization. A new moral system, chivalry, developed at the same time as the Crusades (eleventh–thirteenth centuries). As a code uniting religious and military predilections, it profoundly affected aristocratic life. Idealizing romantic love, ennobling men and improving the status of women, encouraging cleanliness, witty conversation, elegance, and courteous manners, it influenced castle social life, including the taste for art songs and refined social dances. Thus, "minstrels and jugglers had progressively relinquished their monkeys and their bears, concentrating on refining their skills as dancers and choreographers to suit the demands of a more polished and sophisticated society."[8]

By the early fifteenth century, a distinction was made between those musicians who played a treble fiddle and instructed dancing and those who played a bass fiddle in a band. Both the minstrel–dancers and the band members remained within the same guild, headed by the "king of the violins."[9] Indeed, the violin, played by the dancing master himself, continued to be the instrument for accompanying dance classes and ballet lessons until the twentieth century.

## SOCIAL AND THEATRICAL DANCES OF THE RENAISSANCE

This brings us once again to Domenico da Piacenza, author of *De arte saltandi e choreas ducendii*, the earliest extant dance instruction manuscript. Like his French counterparts, Domenico was skilled both in music and dance. The content of his manual, like that of many in the next centuries, gives us an idea of the skills and duties expected of dancing masters at court. For instance, they were theoreticians: "Dancing is the synthesis of movement and space and music

. . . if you do justice to these elements, the result will be true dancing. . . ." But if not, Domenico goes on to say, you will not be more than a "mere stamper of the feet."[10]

Besides giving daily dance instruction to their noble patrons, dancing masters, regarded as experts on proper social behavior, also taught correct ballroom manners, including how to dress properly, how to bow correctly, and how to handle one's gloves, hat, fan, or sword with ease. All were requisites for advancement in courtly circles. We might call this elegant, effortless-looking deportment the "courtesy of grand manners," an attribute still reflected today in the posture and bearing of the classically trained ballet dancer.

The dancing master was expected to devise new dances for the ballroom and for court festivals, where he might also perform along with his noble pupils. Choreographies were documented in a variety of ways: explanations in prose, shorthand symbols, and initial letters or abbreviations of step names. Fifteenth-century French sources depict the elegant, gliding *basse danse*, performed by one couple or by several partners in procession. Despite a limited vocabulary of five movements (*révérence*, single, double, *reprise*, and *branle*), *basses danses* had subtle and sophisticated performance qualities. The Italian counterpart, the *bassadanza*, offered more variety in choreographic pattern, step sequence, and number of participants. Even greater variation was achieved in the *ballo*, a dance piece for a specified number of dancers, featuring frequent changes of musical rhythm and sometimes possibilities for dramatic expression.

Italian festival art developed the *intermezzi*, spectacular musico-dramatic interludes inserted between the acts of lengthy plays. Originating in the late fifteenth century in Ferrara, the *intermezzi* came to include elaborate mechanical marvels of scenic effects; brilliantly costumed actors, singers, and dancers; and the coordinated efforts of poets, composers, designers, and choreographers. During the sixteenth century, thematic material for the *intermezzi* (usually four to six in number) became more unified and sometimes related directly to the play. Their chief purposes, however, were to edify and entertain the spectators and to enhance the prestige of the host. The most elaborate examples were the *intermezzi* of 1589, devised to accompany the comedy *La Pellegrina*, one of the entertainments among the wedding festivities in Florence for Ferdinando de' Medici and Christine of Lorraine. Overseeing the entire production was Emilio de' Cavalieri, a composer, organist, voice teacher, dancer, choreographer, administrator, and diplomat! His choreographic instructions for the final *ballo* (for four women, three men, and a singing chorus that also moved) have survived, providing a rare example of sixteenth-century theatrical dance.

The step vocabulary used by Cavalieri can be understood from published descriptions of similar movements by other Italian dancing masters of the period, notably Fabritio Caroso (*Il ballarino*, Venice, 1581, and *Nobiltà di dame*, Venice, 1600) and Cesare Negri (*Le gratie d'amore*, Milan, 1602). Their treatises include choreographies for dozens of social dances (Negri also has a few theat-

Handsome dance manuals such as *Le gratie d'amore*
("The graces of love," 1602) by Cesare Negri docu-
ment the highly developed dance technique of Italian
courtiers, who practiced intricate legwork while
holding on to pieces of furniture.

COURTESY OF THE BROUDE BROTHERS, LTD., FACSIMILE
EDITION.

rical ones), written in prose form, and their music, written in lute tablature.
Typically beginning and ending with a gracious *riverenza* or bow, the repertory
includes examples of the *balletto*, a couple dance with several sections in contrasting rhythm. An introductory passage, perhaps a stately *pavana* in duple
meter (two or four beats to a bar of music), is followed by a triple-meter
*gagliarda*, in which first the gentleman does a solo of leaps, beats, and jumps
and then the lady performs a variation in a more restrained yet lively manner.
A brisker *saltarello* for both dancers leads to the finale, the exuberant *canario*
with toe–heel brushes and stamps in intricate rhythms.[11]

The structure for such sixteenth-century *balletti* for a *cavalière* and his lady
is not unlike that of the ballet *pas de deux* for a *danseur* and ballerina. Beginning as it does with an *entrée* and *adagio* for the couple, the *pas de deux*
proceeds to exciting variations performed first by the male dancer and then by
his partner and is brought to conclusion in the lively coda for both. The technique is markedly different, however. Renaissance dancers did not point the feet
or turn out the legs. Dancing side-by-side or face-to-face, partners seldom
touched except for an occasional holding or tapping of hands. Indeed, only
movements for the legs are described in this period. Their intricacy, however,
required practice, and Negri's illustrations show a courtier holding onto a table
and a chair, the better to execute his leg movements.

Judging by engravings of the *intermezzi*, theatrical dances for joyous, peaceful scenes were symmetrical and orderly, no doubt performed with the effortless grace espoused for proper social dancing. By contrast, inferno scenes show disorganized, irregular groupings. We can only conjecture what the movement might have been for grotesque or for humorous interludes. Court choreographers may have gleaned ideas from groups of itinerant entertainers, practitioners of *commedia dell'arte* ("comedy of skill") that originated about the mid-sixteenth century. Often parodying court behavior, these professional actors were skilled musicians and dancers as well. Their dynamic quality and popular stock characters, such as Harlequin and Columbine, appear as frequent influences in ballet's technical and artistic history, but documentation of their early dances does not remain.

Lost, too, are the genuine early folk dances of peasants, artisans, and villagers, for the material in the dance manuals reflects only the practice of the courts and upper classes. Yet, through the years, folk and national dances have been lively sources for ballet choreographers to call on. Some vestige of their quality in the Renaissance comes from *Orchesography*, published in 1589 by Thoinot Arbeau, a pseudonym for Jehan Tabourot, a canon in the Roman Catholic Church at Langres. Neither a dancing master nor employee of a royal patron, this scholarly churchman nevertheless wrote an important instruction book of dances standard with the gentry and nobility of the French provinces. Far less complex than the Italian repertory, some of the dances, the many *branles*, for example, may have an even more humble background. Performed with simple steps and hops in a circle or chain formation by several couples, the *branles* may be descendants of the medieval *carole* or *chorea*. Another dance described by Arbeau, the *volta* ("turning"), is a variation of the *galliard* but is distinguished by its hearty turns in which the gentleman lifts his partner.

Arbeau's book, written in the form of a conversation with a student, Capriol, emphasizes courteous social behavior and correct execution of dance technique, including proper positions of the feet and legs. Bearing faint resemblance to ballet's positions of the feet, Arbeau's positions are illustrated showing only slight turnout. He believed that although "the degree [of turnout] is left to the discretion of the dancer . . . the natural rotation of the leg will not permit it to exceed a right angle."[12] Similar positions were used for fencing, which, along with dancing and riding, were requisite accomplishments for any gentleman.

More sophisticated dances were typical of the French royal courts. With the marriage in 1533 of Catherine de Médici, daughter of one of the greatest families of Italy, and Henri, duc d'Orléans, three years later the king of France, Italian dancing masters, employed by the French monarchy, became increasingly important. As queen, and later as queen mother following the untimely death of Henri, Catherine promoted lavish entertainments as much to celebrate events of the royal household as to reinforce her political policies. Costly festivals of several days' duration might include banquets, water shows, firework displays, and balls. Composite entertainments of verse, music, dance, and decor were devised to highlight the occasion. These developed into the genre known as *ballet de cour* ("court ballet"), and, to maximize their effect, they became the responsibility of learned advisors, such as Jean-Antoine de Baif, who advocated the unity of music, verse, and dance—following the example of ancient Greece. To further these goals, a French royal patent in 1570 recognized the efforts of de Baif and his associates by establishing the Académie de Poésie et de Musique.

Three years later, a festival honoring the naming of Catherine's son as king of Poland featured an hour-long ballet devised for sixteen ladies of the court, representing the sixteen provinces of France. Their flawless execution of numerous geometrical patterns so impressed the visiting Polish ambassadors that they declared that no other court on earth could possibly imitate the French dance. The production reflected the work of Baldassare di Belgioioso, who had arrived from Italy in 1555 as a member of a band of violins, and then, changing his name to Beaujoyeulx, became producer of entertainments at Catherine's court.

Perhaps the greatest achievement of Beaujoyeulx and the academicians was the 1581 production of the *Balet Comique de la Royne*, one of many magnificences honoring the marriage of the sister of Catherine's daughter-in-law. According to Beaujoyeulx, the title of the ballet (literally, "The Queen's Comedy-Ballet") was chosen more for the "beautiful, tranquil and happy conclusion than for the quality of the personages, who are almost all gods and goddesses, or other heroic persons."[13]

The plot, a story of the enchantress Circe, whose evil spells finally were broken by intervention of the gods (identified with the royal family), was unfolded by a succession of verses, songs, and dances that gave a certain dramatic unity to the production. The libretto, the music, and several engravings of the elaborate costumes and pageant cars (rather like parade floats, pulled by several men) were published, but, alas, not the choreography. Beaujoyeulx proudly wrote some description of the final dance, however, a *grand ballet* in which ladies of the court performed

> forty passages or geometric figures . . . sometimes square, sometimes round, . . . then in triangles accompanied by a small square. . . . At the middle of the Ballet a chain was formed, composed of four interlacings, each different from the others. . . . The spectators thought that Archimedes[14] could not have understood geometric proportions any better than the princesses and the ladies observed in this Ballet.[15]

Under the influence of the Académie, not only the dance patterns of the ballets but also their steps, music, and verses were closely correlated to produce the greatest symbolic impact, capable of imparting philosophical principles that reinforced the political thrust of the monarchy. "Dancing was no frivolous pastime, but an intensive intellectual experience for both dancer and spectator."[16]

In Italy by the 1580s, permanent theaters were being built, adaptations of earlier Roman designs, with perspective painting added to the stage. Inclined ramps connected the stage to the floor of the auditorium, and all three areas

Members of the aristocracy took part in elaborate court entertainments featuring dancing in intricate geometric patterns as
in this scene from the first *intermezzo of La Liberazione di Tir-
eno e d'Arnea* ("The liberation of Tyrsenus and Arnea," 1617)
held in the Medici theatre of the Uffizi Palace in Florence. Note
the variety of performance levels—auditorium floor, ramps,
stage, and suspended scenery.

COURTESY OF THE DANCE COLLECTION, THE NEW YORK PUBLIC LI-
BRARY AT LINCOLN CENTER, ASTOR, LENOX AND TILDEN FOUNDATIONS.

could be utilized for performance. In France, however, entertainments such as
the *Ballet Comique* occurred in the center floor of large rooms of a palace. Royal
dignitaries sat at one end of the hall, and performers and decorative pageant
cars entered at the opposite end. Along the sides were raised galleries accom-
modating many hundreds of spectators watching the dance patterns unfold.

The English equivalent to the Italian *intermezzi* and the French *ballet de cour*
was the court masque, usually based on a mythological or allegorical theme
adapted to extol the virtues of the monarchy. Enhanced by scenic wonders
devised by stage architect Inigo Jones and verses by poet laureate Ben Jonson,
masques offered a succession of songs, speeches, and dances performed by
elaborately costumed members of the court. Noble, serious characters of the
masque proper were contrasted with demons, furies, and nymphs in anti-
masque sections of the production. Members of the audience were invited to
join the masquers in general dancing, called revels.

Social dancing by the entire assembly frequently terminated theatrical eve-
nings in Italy and France as well. A favorite English form was the country
dance, a lively circle or longways dance for several couples at once. Choreographies and music for these pleasurable dances were collected and published in
1651 in John Playford's *The English Dancing Master*. The English love of dancing
is apparent in the many references to dance by Shakespeare in his plays, such

as in *Henry V* when Bourbon declares, "They bid us to the English dancing schools and teach lavoltas, high and swift corantos." However, during the Commonwealth following the overthrow of the English monarchy in 1640, theatrical activities and court masques were suspended. Italian taste turned to the development of opera, an outgrowth of the *intermezzi*. But in France, the ballet was to enter an important new phase.

## BIRTH OF THE CLASSICAL BALLET

The long reign of Louis XIV (1643–1715) brought *ballet de cour* to its most brilliant phase but also contributed to its demise in favor of the establishment of a fully professional theatrical enterprise. The king, himself a nimble dancer appearing in court ballets over a period of eighteen years and continuing daily dance lessons for many more, excelled as patron of the arts. In bringing together and encouraging first-rate composers, choreographers, dancers, designers, and poets, the royal dancer-patron-impresario intended that court functions would provide a diverting occupation for his courtiers and an impressive display of French cultural magnificence for all Europe.

An early and crucial appointment was that of Jean-Baptiste Lully as composer responsible for the music for court ballets. Having learned to play the guitar in his native Italy, Lully arrived in France as a young teenager and soon showed prowess as violinist and dancer, attracting notice by the court. He danced alongside the young Louis in an elaborate fête, the *Ballet de la Nuit*, in which the fourteen-year-old king first appeared in the role of Apollo, the sun god. A sumptuous example of *ballet à entrée*, the production had four acts, each with a separate plot, composer, and numerous *entrées* ("entrances") interspersed with spoken lines. Typically, most dancers were members of the court. Gradually, as Lully was granted more control, court productions became more integrated unities, and professional dancers, including women, assumed more roles. One virtuoso dancer (and accomplished violinist as well), Pierre Beauchamps, was to have an important place in ballet's formative years.

Beauchamps made his debut as a choreographer in 1661 in the *comédie-ballet*, *Les Facheux* ("The Bores"), a new theater form created by Jean-Baptiste Poquelin, better known by his stage name, Molière. Intending to have dances during the intervals of the acts of his verse play, but given only two weeks to mount the production, Molière instead decided that "in order not to break the thread of the comedy by these sorts of *intermèdes*, it was thought judicious to tack them on to the subject and to make one thing of the ballet and the play. . . ."[17] Thus did expediency lead Molière and Beauchamps, who also composed the music, to use dance as a means of enhancing the actual development of the plot, not merely as a diversion, and to encourage dancers to be more expressive in their dancing, as well as to gesture and pose appropriately during the action of the play. It was a course they followed in other productions, *Le*

*Bourgeois Gentilhomme* ("The Gentleman Citizen," 1670) being probably best known today, but seldom performed with its music or dance possibilities.

In 1661, the year of Louis XIV's ascension to absolute power, the king showed his concern with raising the quality of dancing by establishing the Académie Royale de Danse. Thirteen of the most experienced dancing masters were appointed to set artistic standards for teaching and training dancers for court ballets. Granted independent power to license teachers, the academicians were violently opposed by the musicians' guild, to which dancers had belonged for three centuries. A deeper issue was the divorce of the arts from one another, breaking the unity espoused by Renaissance philosophers.

Creation of dance specialists was deemed timely, however, as ballets took on greater theatrical aspects. One of these was the moving of ballet productions from the ballroom floor onto a raised stage. Giacomo Torelli, an Italian scene designer invited to work at the court in Paris, advocated establishment of the proscenium arch as a stage frame enhancing his use of machines to shift scenes quickly. Such a theater, the Palais Royale, was given over for performances by the Académie Royale de Musique, a performing institution (later known as the Paris Opéra) established by Louis XIV in 1672 to be headed by his protégé, Lully. Pierre Beauchamps, by now director of the dancers' academy, was appointed dancing master to the music academy.

Performers, no longer surrounded by their audience, needed to rely less on symbolic formations of large groups and more on the agility and design of an individual body watched by spectators out front. Precise movements and poses required more codification of the step vocabulary. The establishment of the five positions for the feet, still foundational for today's ballet technique, is credited to Beauchamps, who "found that nothing was more important to maintain the body in a graceful attitude and the steps in a fixed space than to introduce these five positions."[18] Basic to their design was turnout of the leg, already a requirement for "a handsome carriage of the leg . . . regarded as a necessity of elegant bearing" among seventeenth-century nobility and gentry, as well as dancers.[19] The angle of turnout, when heels touched and toes turned outward, was about 90 degrees. Complete 180-degree turnout was still a century away.

Preservation of choreography continued to be a problem, and Louis XIV requested Beauchamps, who had become the monarch's personal dance instructor, to devise a method of notating dance movement. By 1700 the long-awaited notation system was completed and published, not by Beauchamps, however, but by another choreographer, Raoul Anger Feuillet. In his treatise *Chorégraphie*, symbols rather than words indicated positions, steps, and the various movements of the dance: *plié, élevé, sauté, cabriole, tombé, glissé, tourné,* as well as cadence or time, and the figure or pattern of the dance. The French terminology of the Académie Royale de Danse became standard for the rest of the Western dance world, but the execution of the various steps has, in most cases, changed considerably. Nevertheless, by means of the notation system and helpful man-

During the seventeenth century, theatrical productions receded behind the confines of the proscenium stage, as in this performance at Versailles. Performers were well aware of the royal personages seated directly opposite stage center. This "comedy in music," *Les Fêtes de l'Amour et de Bacchus* (*"The Festival of Love and Bacchus,"* first presented in 1672 and revived at intervals until 1738), was based on a text by Molière, with music by Lully and dances by Beauchamps.

COURTESY OF THE DANCE COLLECTION, THE NEW YORK PUBLIC LIBRARY AT LINCOLN CENTER, ASTOR, LENOX, AND TILDEN FOUNDATIONS.

uals from the early eighteenth century,[20] the charming dances of that period can be reconstructed with considerable accuracy. Published along with *Chorégraphie* were notations of theatrical dances composed by Feuillet (including a ballet for nine dancers) and ballroom dances by Guillaume Louis Pécour, Beauchamps' successor at the Académie. For the next twenty-five years, annual collections of dances were published and eagerly sought in order to learn the latest ballroom dances, thus preparing for the coming social season, and to keep up with what was happening in theatrical dance.

Dance technique of both amateur and professional remained essentially the same, differing only in the degree of difficulty expected for stage performance. Judging by the elaborate choreography for esteemed performers such as Balon,

141

*Chorégraphie*, the dance notation system published by Feuillet in 1700, was used widely to record dances in the first decades of the eighteenth century. This is the opening section of a *dance à deux* composed by Pécour. Along the track, which shows the pattern the dancers make in space, are the symbols showing the kinds of steps the dancers make.

FROM THE FACIMILE EDITION BY BROUDE BROTHERS LIMITED. REPRODUCED BY ARRANGEMENT WITH THE PUBLISHER.

Blondy, and Marcel or Mlles Subligny, Guiot, and Prévost, the technical level for ballet was indeed high. Difficult maneuvers of acrobatic nature were depicted in Gregorio Lambranzi's *New and Curious School of Theatrical Dancing* (Nurenberg, 1716).

By the time notated dances appeared, the noble and intellectually demanding *courante*, favorite of Louis XIV, had been replaced in popularity by the livelier, but still subtle and elegant, *minuet*.[21] Theatrical dances included these and other social dance forms, such as *gigues, canaries, sarabandes, gavottes*, and *bourrées*. *Contredanses*, the French embellishment on English country dancing, gained in popularity in the ballroom. Over 350 notated dances exist from the Baroque period and can be reconstructed today.

Movements for the hands and rules for opposition of arms to legs became standardized. Indeed, such were the regulations and influence established by the Paris Opéra throughout Europe that it is not surprising to learn there were rumblings of discontent.

## EIGHTEENTH-CENTURY PROFESSIONALISM AND INNOVATION

Stage dancers were now professionals, but their strictly codified movement and costuming continued to reflect their courtly heritage, as did their stage productions. One highly popular performance vehicle of the early part of the century was the opera-ballet, a musical production of singing, dancing, and scenic display, not unlike the court *ballet à entrées*. In works such as *Les Festes Vénitiennes* (1710) with music by André Campra and choreography by Pécour, opera-ballet offered artistic as well as popular appeal. But some innovative dancers and ballet masters envisioned dramatic dance performances without dependence on either words or song to relate a scenario. Such experiments took place outside the Paris Opéra domain.

In 1717 John Weaver, an English dance master and theoretician, attempted a wholly danced drama, the *Loves of Mars and Venus*, as a revival of practices "from the Ancients, in Imitation of their Pantomime."[22] Also in London, a visiting young French dancer of exceptional expressive ability, Marie Sallé, broke several traditions: She challenged the male dominance in choreography by composing the ballet *Pygmalion* (1734), in which she dared challenge standard costuming as well, appearing "without pannier [hoops around the hips], skirt, or bodice, and with her hair down. . . . Apart from her corset and petticoat she wore only a simple dress of muslin draped about her in the manner of a Greek statue."[23] Sallé's reforms were efforts to achieve greater realism and expression in ballet. Her rival for favor among the highly vociferous ballet fans was Marie-Anne de Cupis de Camargo, a highly skilled technician who excelled in steps of virtuosity heretofore usually associated with male dancers.

Of the many ballet masters who challenged the status quo, only Jean Georges Noverre made the effort to publish his complaints and suggestions. His *Lettres sur la danse et sur les ballets* (1760) urged dancers to

> renounce *cabrioles*, *entrechats*, and overcomplicated steps . . . away with those lifeless masks . . . take off those enormous wigs . . . discard the use of those stiff cumbersome hoops. . . . Renounce that slavish routine which keeps your art in its infancy . . . gracefully set aside the narrow laws of a school to follow the impressions of nature. . . .[24]

Even as he quarreled with much of his dance heritage, Noverre, a student of the elegant "god of the dance," Louis Dupré, did not wish to reject all that had gone on before. For instance, "In order to dance well," he said, "nothing is so important as the turning outward of the thigh."[25] But for Noverre, movements

Prior to the French Revolution, a typical eighteenth-century ballet costume for a male dancer included a plumed headdress and a *tonnelet* or wired skirt not unlike the ballet tutu later worn by female dancers. For women, a tightly laced corset, a long skirt held out by wire frames at the hip or along the petticoat, and heeled shoes were deemed suitable for any role.

COURTESY OF THE DANCE COLLECTION, THE NEW YORK PUBLIC LIBRARY AT LINCOLN CENTER, ASTOR, LENOX, AND TILDEN FOUNDATIONS.

of the legs, no matter how brilliant, were only a part of true dancing, where "everything must speak; each gesture, each attitude, each *port de bras* must possess a different expression."[26]

Noverre elaborated his ideas as ballet master in Stuttgart. Later, in Vienna, he collaborated with composer Christoph Gluck, who was experimenting in similar ways in opera. In 1776 the queen of France, Marie Antoinette, a former pupil of Noverre in her native Vienna, succeeded in having Noverre appointed ballet master at the Paris Opéra, a position he had long coveted.

Noverre created some 150 ballets during his long career, but none survive. He disdained notation, but in any case the old Feuillet system, adequate as it was for earlier divertissements, was not able to accommodate the innovations of *ballet d'action*, in which a dramatic plot was conveyed entirely in movement and gesture.

However, a gently comic ballet by one of Noverre's outstanding pupils, Jean Dauberval, has survived. *La Fille Mal Gardée* ("The Ill-Guarded Girl") was produced in Bordeaux just two weeks before the outbreak of the French Revolution in July 1789. This timely ballet featured peasants as heroes and depicted real-life situations using a dance style that blended the academic technique of the time with folk dance elements. The ballet soon enjoyed success on stages from London to St. Petersburg, and it still is performed today, notably by Britain's Royal Ballet, in versions true, though not to Dauberval's original steps, at least to his carefully constructed plot and delightful characters.

The climactic scene of Noverre's dramatic *ballet d'action*, *Jason et Medée*, is shown in a satiric drawing published during its 1781 London season. Gaetano Vestris, celebrated dancer of the noble style, staged the London version and danced the role of Jason, the faithless lover.

COURTESY OF THE DANCE COLLECTION, THE NEW YORK PUBLIC LIBRARY AT LINCOLN CENTER, ASTOR, LENOX, AND TILDEN FOUNDATIONS.

At the close of the eighteenth century, *ballet d'action* had proved it could relate a story without relying on words or song. Dancing was capable of more than mere divertissement within an opera or drama. Ballets could hold the stage alone, even if they were typically given following, or between the acts of, some other theatrical event.

The wearing of masks to help portray characters, a tradition of ancient origin, was abolished by 1772, allowing facial expression to become more important. Fashion implemented by the French Revolution replaced cumbersome courtly dress and rigid corsets with lighter, more flowing costumes based on Greek and Roman drapery. Greater freedom of movement, especially for the upper body and arms, allowed gesture to become "more natural," a goal of the dance innovators.

At La Scala in Milan, Salvatore Viganò extended the ideas of Noverre and Dauberval to include even more individualized expression. Viganò's grandiose conceptions, in which he strove to "involve the heart" as well as please the eyes, attracted strong support from some (Beethoven composed his only ballet score, *The Creatures of Prometheus*, for him); but others, such as composer Rossini, complained that his ballets contained "too much pantomime and not enough dancing."[27]

Dance technique as well as style had been affected by changes in costume. For women especially, shucking of the long hooped skirts allowed freedom of leg movement hitherto impossible, plus the possibility for supported *adagio*, for now their partners could get close enough to hold them. Charles Didelot, a student of Dauberval, extended the concept of partnering, including simple lifts and movements that emphasized strength for the male and lightness for the female. By an ingenious system of almost-invisible wires, his lightly clad dancers could be raised, lowered, or flown across the stage, an apt device for his highly popular ballet *Flore et Zéphyre* (1796), the love story of a nymph and the breeze of the West Wind.

But having discarded heeled shoes in favor of heelless sandals or slippers, dancers were achieving a new elevation on their own. Outstanding for his sensational jumps, beats, and turns was Auguste Vestris, son of the celebrated Gaetano. Unlike his father, who inherited the elegant, noble style of his teacher, Dupré, Auguste excelled in dazzling virtuoso displays of skill. Steps of almost acrobatic nature, once the specialty of only comic or grotesque dancers, are documented in Gennaro Magri's *Trattato teorico-prattico di ballo* ("theoretical and practical treatise of the ballet," Naples, 1779).

The Paris Opéra had long endeavored to enforce strict observance of three distinct dance styles, including designation of proper physique for each. For the noble style, a dancer's structure should be stately and well proportioned because he would be destined for serious, heroic roles, for gods such as Apollo (or Venus, if a woman). The *demi-caractère* dancer could be of medium height, still elegant but adept at a variety of virtuoso styles appropriate for lesser gods such as

Appearing in London in the 1781 season was Gaetano Vestris's son, Auguste, whose technical virtuosity could not be denied even by this English caricature. Through his dazzling performances as a youth and his long career as a teacher, Auguste Vestris exerted a great influence on the development of ballet technique on the eve of the romantic period.

COURTESY OF THE DANCE COLLECTION, THE NEW YORK PUBLIC LIBRARY AT LINCOLN CENTER, ASTOR, LENOX, AND TILDEN FOUNDATIONS.

Mercury or Zéphir. The comic or grotesque dancer could be of indifferent stature, even thickset, but necessarily strong. His roles were of a rustic or pastoral nature and could include steps and dances characteristic of various national or folklore sources.

But, as in the case of Auguste Vestris, who became an influential teacher in the early nineteenth century, such distinctions of the old order were beginning to break down, just as steps and styles were evolving toward a different form. What was yet lacking was the artistic impetus to make use of these newly developing skills.

## THE GOLDEN AGE OF ROMANTIC BALLET

An artistic push did come along; the romantic movement was felt in ballet no less than in literature, music, and painting. For ballet, it was a liberation from strict thematic and technical conventions of previous eras. Basic subjects of romanticism came from the perceived conflicts between beauty and ugliness, good and evil, spirit and flesh. With themes juxtaposing realism and fantasy,

Newly installed gas lighting enhanced the Paris Opéra premiere of Meyerbeer's opera *Robert le Diable* ("Robert the Devil," 1831), especially this ballet scene, in which the ghosts of nuns rise from their graves to lure Robert. Featuring Marie Taglioni in choreography by her father, the opera's ballet scenes were early examples of the romantic era's fascination with the supernatural and exotic, more fully realized by the Taglionis' *La Sylphide* the next year.

COURTESY OF THE DANCE COLLECTION, THE NEW YORK PUBLIC LIBRARY AT LINCOLN CENTER, ASTOR, LENOX, AND TILDEN FOUNDATIONS.

mortal with supernatural, romantic ballet wanted—and had it—both ways: to be a vehicle for a real drama and a showcase for masters of technique.

The aerial flights provided by Didelot's wires were ideal for the spiritual creatures of the new ballets, but dancers wished to create ethereal illusion by their own movements. Because it was the woman who was cast in the role of unattainable supernatural creature, it was she who desired to dance on the least possible earthly surface, the very tips of her toes. But wishing alone would not make it so.

> Paradoxically, Romanticism may have stressed irrational and spontaneous behavior, but the mastery of a structured and rational training method was needed to portray such behavior on stage.[28]

Such a method had been evolving during the last decades of the previous century, but not until 1820 was there "any really valuable literature upon the subject of dancing." So said the young dancer Carlo Blasis in his *Elementary Treatise upon the Theory and Practice of the Art of Dancing*,[29] the first published account of ballet technique as we recognize it today, including the first outline of the structure of a ballet class. Blasis, who had worked with Dauberval and

Viganò, urged dancers to "be as light as possible. . . . I would like to see you bound with a suppleness and agility which gives me the impression you are barely touching the ground and may at any moment take flight."[30] And his rigorous method of training made the impossible happen. As described in more detail by his disciple, Giovanni Léopold Adice,[31] Blasis's *barre* work included, in the order given, 48 *pliés*, 128 *grand battements*, 96 *petits battements* (like *battements tendus* today), 128 *ronds de jambe à terre* and the same *en l'air*, 64 slow *petits battements sur le cou-de-pied*, and 120 rapid ones. These were "preliminary" exercises, to be repeated in center floor before going on to the rest of the lesson!

Illustrations in Blasis's *Treatise* and his later *Code of Terpsichore* (London, 1828) show dancers in complete 180-degree turnout but, surprisingly, no dancer on full point. Yet prints from the turn of the nineteenth century depict such dancers as Fanny Bias, Amalia Brugnoli, and Maria De (or Del) Caro poised on the extreme points of their toes. But point work as such was not generally in use, nor was its revolutionary nature fully realized. E. A. Théleur, an English dancer and teacher who trained in France and Frenchified his name from Taylor,

*Coll. of Miss Lillian Moore*

Amalia Brugnoli was among the first to dance on the point of her foot, performing "very extraordinary things," according to Marie Taglioni, who saw her in 1822. Brugnoli, shown here with her husband, dancer–choreographer Paolo Samengo, also studied and danced with Carlo Blasis, whose school at La Scala produced many of the extraordinary technicians of nineteenth-century ballet.

COURTESY OF THE DANCE COLLECTION, THE NEW YORK PUBLIC LIBRARY AT LINCOLN CENTER, ASTOR, LENOX, AND TILDEN FOUNDATIONS.

indicated several movements that could be done either "on the balls of the feet or the tips of the toes." His book *Letters on Dancing* (London, 1831)[32] is the first ballet instruction text to actually show illustrations of women on toetip, and it is the first nineteenth-century attempt to devise a new system of dance notation. Like Blasis before, Théleur asserts that heels should never leave the floor in *pliés* and advocates the correct maximum height of the leg as hip level.

This was the training typical at the time Marie Taglioni prepared for her debut in 1822. Arduously trained by her father, Filippo, Marie Taglioni epitomized the newly developing style: Her delicate *piqué* to full point replaced the deliberate rise to half-toe of the previous century; one leg extended slightly backward became a waist-high *arabesque* and, with the other foot poised *en pointe*, a symbolic yearning to soar upward. To the previous emphasis on *terre à terre* steps ("ground-to-ground," meaning the feet scarcely leave the floor) was added the *ballonnée* style with its high and effortless-appearing jumps and leaps.

To show off his daughter's superb skills, Filippo Taglioni created many ballets, including his masterpiece, *La Sylphide* (Paris, 1832), a story of a desirable but unreachable sylph pursued by an infatuated young Scotsman, who, hapless mortal that he was, inadvertently killed his beloved. In the soft glow of gaslights, Taglioni, clothed in a full skirt of the lightest gauze reaching to mid-calf, seemed to float about the huge opera house stage with her soaring, silent *jetés*, her incredibly smooth movements and delicate balances. The theme and setting of *La Sylphide* and the costume, technique, and personality of Marie Taglioni ushered in the golden age of romantic ballet and created a style still popular today. One of the most frequently performed ballets in America has been *Les Sylphides*, a neoromantic storyless ballet created by Michel Fokine to the music of Chopin seventy-six years after *La Sylphide*.

A ballerina is never without rivals, and there were many who wished to share the spotlight with Taglioni. One of the most successful challengers was Fanny Elssler, a Viennese beauty whose specialty was a kind of theatrical folk dancing, done with the sparkle and precision of a highly skilled ballet dancer. Perhaps her greatest success was in *La Cachucha*, a Spanish-style dance that much later was notated by Friederich A. Zorn in *Grammar of the Art of Dancing* (Odessa, 1887). (Spanish influences had been felt in social and theatrical dancing since the Renaissance; ballet dancers routinely played castanets.) When Taglioni accepted an invitation to dance in St. Petersburg, Elssler remained in Paris to enjoy the role of undisputed star of the Opéra. Two years later, in 1840, Elssler crossed the Atlantic for a three-month American tour that was extended to two years. Audiences in New York, Philadelphia, and Baltimore rivaled each other in their adulation for Elssler and her fiery dances; Congress adjourned for her performances in Washington.

The spiritual Taglioni and the sensual Elssler split the artistic world of ballet fans into two passionate factions, reminiscent of the Sallé-Camargo rivalry a century before. But another ballerina came along who offered the public *both*

Fanny Elssler charmed audiences in the United States as well as in all of Europe with her passionate dancing, especially in *La Cachucha* (1836), a Spanish-style solo complete with castanet playing. This portrait accompanied the New York publication of the sheet music for that dance.

AUTHOR'S COLLECTION.

qualities, moreover in the same ballet; she was Carlotta Grisi, and the ballet was *Giselle*. First performed in 1841, *Giselle* is a universally touching story with a role that tempts, and thereby challenges, every ballerina. It tells of a simple peasant girl, Giselle, who is betrayed in love, goes mad with grief, and kills herself. But that is only Act I. By Act II, Giselle has become one of the Wilis, the spirits of betrothed girls who have died as maidens. At midnight the Wilis rise from their graves to attract young men into their midst, only to compel them to dance until they fall dead with exhaustion. But Giselle saves her deceitful (now repentant) lover from such a fate by offering to dance in his place. This scenario was developed from an old German legend by several men, including Théophile Gautier, a poet turned ballet critic, whose great admiration for Carlotta Grisi glowed from his windy, flowery reviews. Jean Coralli did the choreography, with solo passages for Mlle Grisi composed by Jules Perrot, one of the few male dancers of the romantic era to receive much attention from the public or press, although his contributions to *Giselle* went unacknowledged at the time. Adolphe Adam composed a score that gave leading characters identifiable melodic themes throughout the ballet.

An American dancer, Mary Ann Lee, traveled to Europe to study and then returned to dance *Giselle* in Boston in 1846. Her partner was George Washington Smith, the first American *premier danseur*. Their contemporary, Augusta Maywood, extended a European visit to a lifetime career, becoming the first American dancer to achieve fame and fortune abroad.

The ballerina had become the undisputed star of the ballet stage. Four of these talented, temperamental ladies were persuaded to dance together in 1845. Their short ballet, *Pas de Quatre*, was a masterpiece of choreographic diplomacy by Perrot, who managed to display the individual skills of the dancers without offending the pride of any one of them. It was agreed that Taglioni should be awarded the place of honor, the final variation of the ballet. The others, after tempestuous argument on the day of the performance, finally agreed to appear in order of their age: first, the young Danish ballerina Lucile Grahn, who excelled in *pirouettes*, then Carlotta Grisi, followed by Fanny Cerrito, an Italian dancer of uncommon speed and brilliance.

These and other ballerinas continually expanded the limits of ballet technique. They rivaled male dancers in the size of their leaps and the speed of their footwork. They danced more and more on the tips of their toes, an achievement requiring tremendous strength in soft slippers. A little darning around the point of the shoe, a little cotton batting inside, and ribbons tied tightly around the ankles offered the only assistance to Taglioni and others of her era. The delicately pale, unworldly romantic ballerina was, in fact, a far stronger technician than her robust, voluptuous eighteenth-century predecessor. For the first time in the history of Western theatrical dancing, females, now *en pointe*, replaced males as the dominant stage performers. However, two male dancer-choreographers of the period deserve special mention: Auguste Bournonville, developer of the Danish repertory, and Arthur Saint-Léon, creator of *Coppélia* and a system of dance notation.

Bournonville studied with Auguste Vestris. Through his many ballets still performed today by the Royal Danish Ballet and by his documentation of ballet technique in *Études chorégraphiques* (Copenhagen, 1861), Bournonville is responsible for keeping alive much of the French ballet tradition. His version of *La Sylphide*, not Taglioni's, is the one usually seen today. Bournonville should not be accused of plagiarism; adapting someone else's ballet, without necessarily giving

Jules Perrot's plotless divertissement *Pas de Quatre* (1845) cleverly displayed the individual skills of four of the greatest ballerinas of the romantic period, shown here in the pose with which the ballet began and ended. Surrounding Marie Taglioni are Carlotta Grisi, Lucile Grahn, and Fanny Cerrito.

COURTESY OF THE DANCE COLLECTION, THE NEW YORK PUBLIC LIBRARY AT LINCOLN CENTER, ASTOR, LENOX, AND TILDEN FOUNDATIONS.

credit to the originator or using the original musical score, was a common practice in both the eighteenth and nineteenth centuries.

Saint-Léon's international career was also typical of dancers and ballet masters of the time. He worked in London, St. Petersburg, Rome, Brussels, Milan, and Vienna, as well as his native Paris. Somehow he found time to publish, in 1852, a system of dance notation, *Sténochorégraphie*. Easy to decipher, his notation and descriptions give vivid examples of classroom exercises closely related to the earlier tradition described by Blasis and Théleur, including *grands pirouettes* and multiple beats.

Among the very few notated dances of the first half of the nineteenth century are the *Gavotte de Vestris*, an already famous duet by the time Théleur notated it, and a *pas de six* from *La Vivandière*, one of Saint-Léon's popular ballets and his only piece he succeeded in recording. Sad to say, most of the great romantic ballet repertory has been forgotten, and the rest has survived only through fallible memory.

In the second half of the nineteenth century, the great opera houses of Europe relied more and more on spectacular vehicles tailored for the talents of a star ballerina. Smaller provincial theaters, unable to satisfy public taste for such elaborate fare, gradually ceased sponsoring new ballet productions, thus drying up a traditional source for inventive choreography. The lack of fine roles for male dancers and public preference for female dancers resulted in women taking male roles *en travestie*. The role of Franz in *Coppélia*, for instance, was originated by the shapely Eugénie Fiocre, a tradition for that ballet that continued well into this century.

London, once an ardent sponsor of the finest ballets at Her Majesty's Theatre, began to relegate dancing to divertissements during intervals between other acts at the Alhambra and Empire music halls. In Copenhagen, Bournonville managed to preserve the artistry of the romantic period, avoiding excesses he observed elsewhere: the ". . . unending and monotonous host of feats of bravura . . . obvious lascivious tendency that pervades the whole choreographic movement . . . heroines of the ballet continuously appear in the same more or less spangled costume. . . ."[33] His comments referred to the Russian repertory of the 1870s, before it entered a period of brilliant successes that in many ways marked the glorious culmination of the romantic era.

## EMERGENCE OF BALLET IN RUSSIA

The Russian theater had long relied on foreign talent for its ballet, beginning in the eighteenth century with imported French ballet masters Jean-Baptiste Landé and Charles LePicq and with exponents of *ballet d'action* from Vienna, Franz Hilverding and Gasparo Angiolini. At the start of the nineteenth century, Didelot came to St. Petersburg, revolutionizing teaching methods and establishing the foundation of the Russian school. His work was continued by his fellow countrymen Perrot and Saint-Léon. Still another Frenchman, Marius Petipa, was to have the greatest effect. Arriving in St. Petersburg in 1847 at age twenty-five, he was to become *premier danseur* and then ballet master of the Imperial Ballet. By the end of his remarkable fifty-six-year career in Russia, Petipa had created close to sixty ballets and so nurtured native Russian talent that his adopted country, and in due time the world, was convinced that the very best in ballet meant Russian ballet.

A Petipa production meant evening-length ballets of several acts, fantastic stage effects, and fairy-tale plots related through pantomimic gestures by characters whose natures were revealed through their dances. Diversity during the long evening was achieved by alternating acts having naturalistic settings, which might include lively comic or folk dance–inspired passages, with acts having supernatural locations, perhaps a dream sequence with enchanted, winged creatures. Beautiful symmetry characterized a Petipa ballet — groups of four, eight, thirty-two, or more lovely women moving in ingenious patterns. Dance passages often were repeated three times, then brought to an appropriately bravura finish. The hero and heroine usually performed only in the nobler, classical style, and their *pas de deux* was the highlight of any given act. With Petipa, the *grand pas de deux* — *adagio*, variations, and coda — reached a level of artistry that is still much admired, remaining technically challenging as well. Some Petipa repertory was preserved in a system of notation devised by Vladimir Stepanov and later used to mount the ballets in the West. One of these, *The Sleeping Beauty*, produced in 1890, was perhaps Petipa's crowning achievement. Its scenario was meticulously outlined by Petipa for Tchaikowsky, whose score is considered one of the finest.

It would be unfair to leave the impression that Marius Petipa singlehandedly made Russia the ballet capital of the world, for he had help from many sources. His talented but humble assistant, Lev Ivanov, was responsible for choreography of *The Nutcracker* and for Acts II and IV of *Swan Lake*, two other ballets with music by Tchaikowsky that probably are the most popular works associated with ballet from the 1890s. Christian Johannsen, a pupil of Bournonville who was already a leading dancer with the Imperial Ballet when Petipa first arrived, later became one of the finest teachers of its school. In the latter part of the century, the Imperial Theatre was host to a galaxy of Italian stars, products of the Blasis tradition of rigorous schooling. Among them were Virginia Zucchi and Pierina Legnani, whose amazing technique (including Legnani's sensational thirty-two *fouettés*) was carefully studied and then emulated by Russian dancers. Another technical wizard from Italy, Enrico Cecchetti, became an invaluable teacher in Russia before bringing his influential method of instruction to the West.

With the graduation of Olga Preobrajenska in 1889 and of Mathilde Kchessinska the following year, the Imperial Theatre School produced two native dancers as glorious as the foreign artists who had so long monopolized the

Russian ballet spotlight. They were only the first of many. Imagine the excitement of classrooms where pupils such as Anna Pavlova, Tamara Karsavina, and Michel Fokine came from childhood on for their daily lessons. A class of perfection was established for such outstanding artists of the school. Nicolas Legat succeeded his master, Johannsen, as instructor, and accounts of his teaching can be found in *Heritage of a Ballet Master: Nicolas Legat*,[34] by one of his pupils, André Eglevsky, later a soloist with the New York City Ballet.

Ballet at the Imperial Theatre (renamed the Maryinsky; today known as the Kirov) was the pride of the czars, whose purse generously funded it. Productions at the lesser-renowned Bolshoi Theatre in Moscow grew in importance under the leadership of Alexander Gorsky.

By the end of the nineteenth century, dancers and audiences had grown accustomed to a kind of ballet ritual revolving around bravura technique. A slightly stiffer ballet slipper was developed that allowed the ballerinas to try more and more difficult steps on point. Male dancers regularly performed eight or more spins (*pirouettes*) and multiple crossings (*entrechats*) of the legs while in the air. Solo dances stopped the show, and the excitement was so great that even a ballerina's entrance was greeted with applause. Indeed she was an impressive sight, with diamonds sparkling from her head, ears, and neck. No matter what her role or the theme of the ballet, a ballerina wore jewels from her private collection (usually gifts from titled admirers) and a full-skirted, tight-waisted costume (*tutu*) that reached to just above her knees. Soloists were allowed to insert their favorite steps into the choreography; they danced along with the music but many considered it an incidental element.

Noverre would have written a manifesto scolding such absurdities just as he did in his own time, almost 150 years before. As it happened, a young Russian dancer and choreographer, Michel Fokine, picked up the pen in 1904 and urged the ballet administration to work for more harmonious productions in which music, decor, costume, and dance would blend in a meaningful way. He decried the gymnastics that had crept into ballet at the expense of a sensitive interpretation of a chosen theme. He believed a mood or story line should be understandable through the dance, rather than dependent on passages of pantomime.

Soon after, Isadora Duncan, a free-spirited American dancer, visited Russia and greatly impressed Fokine, Gorsky, and others with her expressivity, her sensitivity to music, and her revolutionary appearance — bare feet, unbound hair, and flowing Grecian tunic. While the Russians did not wish to emulate Duncan's contempt for the classical ballet, they believed innovative ideas like hers would bring freshness into the static situation in Russian theaters. But management did not approve of suggestions in this direction (Marius Petipa had retired by 1903, but traditions established during his reign continued). Subsequently, a group of Russian artists, including Fokine, determined to bring ballet into the twentieth century and to transport their ideas and talents out of Russia for the rest of the world to appreciate. It was a challenge, and it proved to be their glory.

The one performance in all ballet history that most dancers wish they could have seen occurred in Paris on an evening in May 1909. It was the European debut of the Ballets Russes, the birth of a new era in ballet. Instead of one full-length ballet, the program consisted of several distinctly different offerings, each with its own dance style. The dancing seemed born of the music; the costumes of the moving figures blended into the decor of the stage — it was "total theater," the dream of Michel Fokine brought to reality by a company of young Russians.

At the helm of this historic troupe was Serge Diaghilev, artistic director and impressario extraordinary. Although skilled in neither painting, music, nor dance, he had the capacity to discover and inspire the greatest talents in each of those areas, and he longed to prove the talents of his countrymen — to themselves and to a Europe that had heretofore considered Russia a rather barbaric land. Before the formation of the Ballets Russes, Diaghilev had brought Russian art to Paris galleries, Russian music to its concert halls, and finally a production of *Boris Godunov* to the Paris Opéra itself. The success of these ventures challenged him to test Paris with the outstanding stars of the Russian ballet in productions completely new to Europe.

Diaghilev knew the choreographic potential of Fokine, who was eager to have his ballets staged without the restrictions imposed by the Maryinsky management. The ballets that Diaghilev selected for the Paris season included *Le Pavillon d'Armide*, evoking the gracious style of the court of Louis XIV; *Cléopâtre*, a dramatic vision of ancient Egypt; *Les Sylphides*, a suite of dances in romantic style and costume; and the savage Polovtsian dances from the opera *Prince Igor*. Collaborations were started with St. Petersburg painters Alexandre Benois and Léon Bakst for sets and costumes. Igor Stravinsky was asked to arrange some of the Chopin music for *Les Sylphides*. The Russian theaters agreed to release Fokine and a number of other dancers to go with Diaghilev during the summer months when they were not working. No one has ever assembled a finer roster of dancers, some of whom became legends in their own lifetimes. Leading *danseur* was Vaslav Nijinsky, possessor of an incredible elevation, a magnetic stage personality, and an acting ability that matched his fabulous dance technique. Heading the list of ballerinas was Anna Pavlova, who seemed to epitomize the Fokine philosophy. She had an uncanny ability to use every part of her exquisite body to create a magical image of motion and stillness that seemed beyond the range of mere bones and muscles. For her, Fokine had created *The Swan* (later known as *The Dying Swan*), perhaps the finest dramatic ballet solo ever devised. Among the other stars of that first Paris season were Tamara Karsavina, Vera Fokina (wife of Michel Fokine), Adolph Bolm, and Mikhail Mordkin.

They set out on an unprecedented adventure, meticulously and extravagantly guided by Diaghilev, even to the redecoration of the Théâtre du Châtelet and the seating of the most attractive influential people for that first audience. The season was a triumph. Paris (where the *danseur* was known as a *porteur* because his main function was to lift the ballerina) was astounded by the virile dancing of the Russian men in *Prince Igor*. The bold colors used by Bakst for the decor of *Cléopâtre* were completely new to the Paris stage, as was the total harmony of costumes and sets created by Benois for *Le Pavillon d'Armide* and *Les Sylphides*. Paris was accustomed to a *corps de ballet* that served as little more than living scenery; the Russians instead presented an ensemble of fine dancers, in which each individual contributed to the overall effect. The versatility of all the ballerinas was admired, but Paris was especially captivated by the exotic beauty and dramatic skills of Ida Rubinstein as Cléopâtre.

As the Paris press trumpeted every aspect of the Ballets Russes, its distribution of praise had two monumental effects on the course of ballet history: It tempted Diaghilev to arrange future summer seasons for his ballet company in Europe, and it tempted Pavlova to strike out on her own. Having been offered other engagements outside Russia, she soon left both the Diaghilev company and the Maryinsky Theatre, eventually forming her own company. She became a kind of dance missionary, bringing ballet and her own unique artistry to practically every section of the globe. A whole generation of dancers, would-be dancers, and ballet fans emerged because they "had seen Pavlova." There were few masterpieces in her repertory other than Fokine's *Dying Swan*, but Pavlova, as dragonfly or snowflake or butterfly, infused even inferior choreography and insipid music with a special magic.

The years from 1909 to 1913 marked a period of notable success for all concerned. Diaghilev formed a permanent company, one completely independent from the Russian theaters. The prolific Fokine created *Schéhérazade*, *The Firebird*, *Carnaval*, *Spector of the Rose*, *Daphnis and Chloë*, *Petrouchka*, and eight other ballets of lesser fame. Igor Stravinsky, commissioned to compose music for *The Firebird*, became famous as a result and began his close collaboration with the Diaghilev Ballet. The costumes designed by Léon Bakst for *Schéhérazade* launched a wave of semioriental fashion for Parisian women.

The dancers were continually challenged by new and different roles. With the exit of Pavlova, Karsavina became the leading ballerina. Nijinsky revealed his unique gifts as a choreographer. His four ballets, notably *Afternoon of a Faun* and *The Rite of Spring*, seemed a denial of classical ballet; their angular, "primitive" movements and rhythmic motivation anticipated a vocabulary later developed by such modern dancers as Mary Wigman and Martha Graham.

Much to Diaghilev's pleasure, his troupe produced one novel ballet after another, although not all were successful with the public and the press. Then came 1914 and World War I. Despite the chaos of the times, Diaghilev determined to continue his company. Around a newly discovered choreographic talent, Leonide Massine, a new repertory began to take shape. Promising young dancers were recruited: Stanislas Idzikowski and Leon Woizikowski from Poland and Vera Nemtchinova from Moscow. An English dancer, Hilda Munnings, joined the

Many of the great traditions of nineteenth-century ballet technique and romantic artistry were carried into the twentieth century to nearly all corners of the world by the annual tours of Anna Pavlova, shown here in *The Dying Swan*, a two-minute solo choreographed for her by Fokine in 1905.

COURTESY OF THE DANCE COLLECTION, THE NEW YORK PUBLIC LIBRARY AT LINCOLN CENTER, ASTOR, LENOX, AND TILDEN FOUNDATIONS.

company and was renamed Lydia Sokolova. Cecchetti was engaged to guide these and other young talents in daily classes of strict technique. His method of instruction, including set *adagio* and *allegro* sequences for each day of the week, was compiled in *A Manual of the Theory and Practice of Classical Theatrical Dancing* (London, 1922).[35] Besides Bakst and Stravinsky, there were Michel Larionov, painter, and Ernest Ansermet, conductor. Diaghilev had again assembled a group of extraordinary talents, and the Ballets Russes continued, very like a tiny, independent kingdom of art in the midst of a world at war.

Massine produced several popular ballets in quick succession: *The Good-Humored Ladies*, *La Boutique Fantasque*, and *The Three-Cornered Hat*. His most startling effort was the surrealist ballet *Parade*, with decor and costumes by Picasso. In later years, the choreographic skills of Bronislava Nijinska (sister of Vaslav) and George Balanchine (a 1924 defector from the Soviet Union) were encouraged. Composers who worked with the company included Satie, Poulenc, Milhaud, de Falla, Prokofiev, Ravel, Debussy, and, of course, Stravinsky. In 1928 Stravinsky and Balanchine began a collaboration that extended more than forty

Some of the innovative repertory from Diaghilev's Ballets Russes survived through revivals by subsequent companies. George Zoritch, soloist with Ballet Russe de Monte Carlo and Grand Ballet du Marquis de Cuevas, is pictured here in Fokine's *Le Spectre de la Rose* ("The Spirit of the Rose") created for Nijinsky in 1911.

PHOTO: SERGE LIDO.

years. An early effort, *Apollon Musagète* (now known simply as *Apollo*), introduced a "neoclassical" style in which academic ballet training served as a base for stunning technical innovation.

The Diaghilev stage served as an inviting canvas for such painters as Braque, Picasso, Derain, and Rouault. The roster of dancers was ever-changing and everexciting. Books have been written about many of them, but all deserve at least mention in any historical account. Space limits us merely to listing a few additional names: Spessivtzeva, Lopokova, Dolin, Danilova, Markova, Egorova, Nikitina, Doubrovska, Lifar.

They lived a nomadic and precarious existence, these members of the first great ballet company without backing from a state or royal treasury. Home became Monte Carlo for rehearsal periods and an annual season, but the company existed only from one season to the next, dependent on bookings in Europe, South America, and the United States, on alliances with influential impressarios of opera houses, and on the generosity of wealthy patrons; somehow necessary financing was always secured just in time. For twenty years, the Ballets Russes led the world to a new appreciation of ballet. But it was Diaghilev's company, and with his death in 1929 the organization collapsed, the dancers scattered, and an era ended.

## BALLET AFTER DIAGHILEV

The vision that Diaghilev had was too strong to die completely with him. During the 1930s, there emerged a series of companies whose names incorporated the magic box-office words "Ballet Russe" or "Monte Carlo" and whose repertories preserved many of the great ballets from the Diaghilev years. Massine continued to create remarkable ballets, some to symphonic scores, his lighter works including *Gaité Parisienne* and *Capriccio Espagnol*. The companies included many of the stars from the Diaghilev ballet plus an international list of new talents, such as Igor Youskevitch, Frederic Franklin, George Zoritch, André Eglevsky, Mia Slavinska, and the "baby ballerinas" Toumanova, Riabouchinska, and Baronova.

The constant touring of these companies during the 1930s and 1940s produced a new generation of ballet fans. England and the United States were especially receptive, and serious efforts were made to encourage native talent and establish permanent companies in those countries. No state support for such projects existed in either England or the United States, but by the great determination and dedication of a few persons, companies were formed and, more important, ballet schools were established in both countries.

## BRITISH BALLET

In 1920, Marie Rambert founded a school and began the groundwork for what became Ballet Rambert, now Britain's oldest dance company. Always providing an atmosphere for experimentation, the company gave early choreographic opportunities to Frederick Ashton and Antony Tudor. Since 1966 it has been primarily a modern dance troupe, a reorganization fully endorsed by Rambert, who as a girl had studied eurhythmics, a system of translating musical rhythms into body movements. She used these skills to coach Nijinsky, at Diaghilev's suggestion, in preparation for Stravinsky's challenging score for *Rite of Spring*.

Another grand dream was conceived and carried out by Ninette de Valois, a former student of Cecchetti and dancer with the Diaghilev company. From her London studio, founded in 1926, emerged a company known as the Vic-Wells, then as the Sadler's Wells Ballet when it moved to the theater by that name. The de Valois policy of carefully recreating nineteenth-century classics was epitomized by the revival of the original Petipa version of *Sleeping Beauty*, staged by former Maryinsky dancer Nicholas Sergeyev from the Stepanov notation. It became the company's signature piece, used in a gala performance after World War II for the reopening of the Royal Opera House at Covent Garden, the company's new home, and for its first triumphant New York season in 1949. The role of Princess Aurora in the ballet has been indelibly associated with Margot

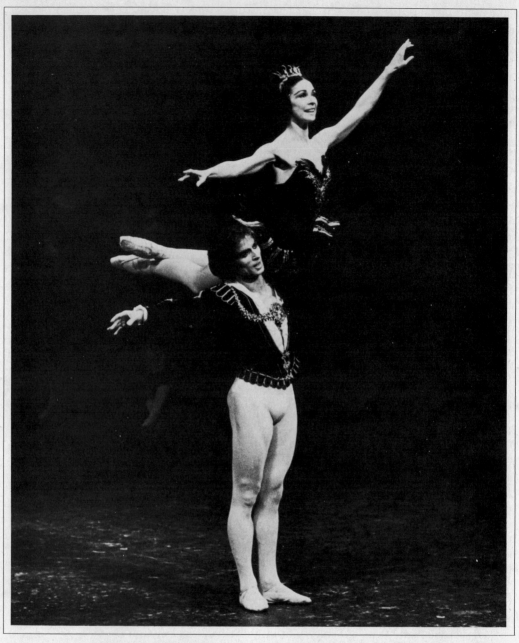

The dynamic partnership of Margot Fonteyn and Rudolf Nureyev, shown here in the "Black Swan" *pas de deux* from Petipa and Ivanov's *Le Lac des Cygnes* ("Swan Lake," 1895) combined the English and Russian ballet traditions to the delight of Western audiences during the 1960s.

PHOTO: JUDY CAMERON.

Fonteyn, a product of the de Valois school, who became one of the world's truly exquisite ballerinas. The company was awarded a royal charter in 1956, thus becoming the Royal Ballet and fulfilling the de Valois dream. Principal choreographer Ashton, and later Kenneth MacMillan, built a balanced repertory of contemporary ballets and new productions of the classics.

Another British institution begun in the 1920s deserves mention in a ballet textbook: the Royal Academy of Dancing (RAD). Its initial purpose was to raise the artistic level of dancing and to improve teaching methods in Britain. Its first syllabus, written by Edouard Espinosa, reflected his French training, but also the Italian, Danish, Russian, and English traditions of the other founding members. Annual examinations, now worldwide, and teachers' training courses continue the ideas of the Academy.

## THE AMERICAN SCENE

Across the Atlantic, performing outlets for American dancers in the early twentieth century included musical revues, vaudeville tours, and occasional concerts by small troupes from local studios — not unlike the dance opportunities in Britain at the time. Opera companies in New York, and later in San Francisco and Chicago, maintained a European repertory and performance model in which, at most, dance was an incidental divertissement. However, a young Harvard graduate, Lincoln Kirstein, envisioned an American ballet company and fortunately had the financial means to implement his plans, for there was no government help, not even, as in most countries, a secretary or minister for the arts. Impressed with the neoclassical choreography of George Balanchine, Kirstein invited the young choreographer to the United States to found a company. Balanchine's famous reply, "But first, a school," resulted in the establishment of the School of American Ballet. In that same year, 1934, Balanchine devised his first American ballet, *Serenade* (to Tchaikowsky's Serenade for String Orchestra), as a study in performance techniques for his students. The school and that particular ballet have flourished to this day, although the company had a rocky start. First called the American Ballet, it operated for a short period as the resident company for the Metropolitan Opera, but Balanchine's disregard for simple, traditional operatic dances upset the directors, singers, and conservative audience and soon finished off the relationship. After periods of little activity and reorganization with another Kirstein group, Ballet Caravan, the company finally in 1948 found a performing home, the New York City Center, and a new name, the New York City Ballet (NYCB).

The company repertory and style have always been dominated by Balanchine, even though Jerome Robbins, an American dancer-choreographer, was added as an associate director. Despite his Maryinsky background, Balanchine choreographed only a few full-length ballets—*Jewels, Don Quixote, A Midsummer Night's Dream*, and a perennially popular version of *The Nutcracker*. Instead, he usually followed the Diaghilev formula of three or four short ballets on each program. But unlike most ballets from the Diaghilev years, the Balanchine selections seldom have a story line or elaborate decor. Music, often an intricate score from Stravinsky, was the catalyst for Balanchine's "pure dance" ballets, usually set on a bare stage and performed with incredible speed and stamina by dancers (most of whom trained in the company school) dressed in tights, leotards, or simple tunics.

Balanchine's 1957 ballet *Agon* packed an unprecedented amount of movement into only twenty minutes. Classical technique was stretched and explored as it never had been before. The complexities of Stravinsky's rhythms and twelve-tone style were matched by Balanchine's twelve disciplined dancers. It was a turning point for ballet, as the Balanchine-Stravinsky *Apollo* had been almost thirty years before.

The company seldom tours, enjoying lengthy seasons and the stability of a home base, now at New York's handsome Lincoln Center for the Performing Arts. City Ballet, as it is familiarly known, has produced many fine male dancers, such as Edward Villella, Jacques d'Amboise, and Arthur Mitchell. But, to most minds, the "Balanchine dancer" is typified by such streamlined ballerinas as Diana Adams, Tanaquil LeClerq, and Maria Tallchief; later, Allegra Kent, Suzanne Farrell, and Patricia McBride; and more recently, Kyra Nichols and Darci Kistler, who at age eighteen became the youngest principal dancer in the company's history. All have performed with pistonlike point work and limber, over-the-head extensions, technical attributes now expected by most companies, many of whom have added Balanchine ballets to their repertories. Danish-trained principal dancer Peter Martins has gained critical acclaim for his choreography, building on the Balanchine model but promising to carve out a distinctive style of his own. In 1983 George Balanchine died, and Martins and Robbins were given responsibility for the operation of the company.

American Ballet Theatre (ABT) has followed quite a different path. Founded by Lucia Chase and Richard Pleasant, the company, until 1957 known simply as Ballet Theatre, has, from its opening season in 1940, been a kind of touring library of ballet. Its repertory tries to remain as strong in revived or revised classics as it is in works of established contemporary choreographers, both American and foreign, and in the experimental attempts of newcomers. Opportunities given to Agnes De Mille, Jerome Robbins, Michael Kidd, and Herbert Ross resulted in exciting, often-masterful ballets.

At the invitation of Ballet Theatre, Antony Tudor came to America from England and brought a new dimension for ballet. It has been called a psychological element, for Tudor dealt with the motivations and emotions of ordinary people—their hopes, their struggles, their foibles—replacing the stylized poses of classical technique with natural gestures. Rejecting dance-for-dance's-sake, he offered instead a continuous flow of movement that carries the action of ballet to its inevitable conclusion. Tudor required that his dancers be fine actors as well as strong technicians—a challenge met especially well by Nora Kaye, Hugh

A *pas de deux* from the Balanchine/Stravinsky collaboration *Agon* ("Contest," 1957) is pictured as performed by its original New York City Ballet cast, Arthur Mitchell and Diana Adams. This plotless ballet, with its revealing classroom dress and its exploration of the technical range and complexity possible within the ballet medium, has had great impact on subsequent productions and perhaps even on ballet training.

PHOTO: MARTHA SWOPE.

Laing, and Sallie Wilson. In 1942 Ballet Theatre produced Tudor's *Pillar of Fire*, the story of Hagar, who, fearful that she will be a spinster like her older sister, has an affair with a young man and then later finds forgiveness and peace with the one she had loved earlier. *Pillar of Fire* became an immediate success, assuring a prominent place for the ballet with a psychological theme.

Offering perhaps the most varied repertory of any company in the world (as many as sixty ballets by thirty different choreographers in a single season) and promoting guest artists, ABT has long attracted ballet superstars from Alicia Alonso (Cuba) to Erik Bruhn (Denmark), and more recently Natalia Makarova (Soviet Union). Another Soviet expatriate, Mikhail Baryshnikov, joined Makarova as a member of the company, becoming its artistic director in 1980. Baryshnikov's own high level of virtuosity has given a new boost to traditional ballet roles and to the technique itself. Dance critic Arlene Croce expresses it well:

> For Baryshnikov, a double *pirouette* or air turn is a linking step, and preparations barely exist. . . . He also performs invented steps. One is a turning *jeté* in which, at the last second, he changes the foot he's going to land on and his legs flash past each other in the air. . . . Baryshnikov's promise lies not in novel steps but in his power to push classical steps to a new extreme in logic, a new density of interest. He is a modern classical dancer.[36]

ABT continues to encourage choreographic innovation and technical expansion, as in, for example, its sponsorship of modern dance renegade Twyla Tharp's witty, unconventional compositions. Her 1976 ballet for ABT, *Push Comes to Shove*, both mocked and praised classical ballet and provided Baryshnikov with one of his most memorable and challenging roles. In 1988 Tharp became an Artistic Associate of the company, bringing several of her own dancers into an ever-more-eclectic ABT.

## BALLET ECLECTICISM AND TRADITIONALISM

Early in the twentieth century, some American dancers believed the codified technique and Russo-European traditions of ballet were an inappropriate and inadequate means of expression for their country and their time. Such persons were called "modern" dancers because, following the inspiration of Isadora Duncan, they broke with all traditional forms in an effort to devise a more contemporary dance expression.

A school and company called Denishawn were established in Los Angeles in 1915 by two pioneers of the new dance, Ruth St. Denis and her husband Ted Shawn. Oddly enough, St. Denis found many of her movement themes in religious dances of the Orient. Shawn, on the other hand, filled his dances with Americana, using subjects and styles he believed were especially suited to the male dancer—American Indians, laborers, farmers, athletes. From the amalgam that was the Denishawn group came Martha Graham, Doris Humphrey, and Charles Weidman, all of whom founded companies of their own and eventually evolved movement principles on which new dance techniques were built.

Nigel Courtney seems to fly across stage as Ariel in *The Tempest*, a full-length ballet based on Shakespeare's play. Created in 1980 for the San Francisco Ballet by then codirector Michael Smuin, the ballet transferred successfully to the television screen for the *Dance in America* series.

PHOTO: RUDI LEGNAME.

Their influence was felt in ballet circles, where choreographers began to look for subject matter from their native land and movements that would appropriately illustrate those themes. Among the first successful ballets of this type were *Filling Station* by Lew Christensen and *Billy the Kid* by Eugene Loring, both produced in 1938 by Ballet Caravan. The Wild West was the inspiration of another popular work a few years later, *Rodeo*, by Agnes De Mille. Jerome Robbins, like De Mille, brought to ballet choreography a varied background — ballet, modern, jazz, tap — that he brilliantly wove into a little masterpiece, *Fancy Free*, the saga of three sailors on leave in Manhattan, set to a new jazz score by Leonard Bernstein in 1944.

New York became the dance capital of the United States, but ballet activity had spread from coast to coast. The San Francisco Ballet celebrated its fiftieth anniversary in 1983, making it the oldest professional company in the country. Emerging as a separate entity from the San Francisco Opera, the company, under the leadership of William Christensen, in 1940 offered the first full-length production of *Swan Lake* staged by an American. One of the company's box office successes of the 1990s is its new production of *Swan Lake* staged by the current company artistic director, Helgi Tomasson, former soloist with NYCB.

## TODAY'S BALLET

Although American ballet has decentralized, many, perhaps most, of its regional professional companies are highly influenced by the legacy of George Balanchine and the New York City Ballet. Former NYCB dancers who have

Oakland Ballet, under the artistic leadership of director Ronn Guidi, has in its repertory a number of ballets originally created for Diaghilev's Ballets Russes. A 1989 addition was Bronislava Nijinska's *Le Train Bleu* (1924), staged and directed by her daughter, Irina Nijinska, and dance historian Frank W. D. Ries. The original collaborators included Darius Milhaud (music), Jean Cocteau (libretto), and Gabrielle "Coco" Chanel, who designed the all-wool bathing suits. Pictured here are Oakland Ballet dancers Abra Rudisill and Michael Lowe as members of the young fashionable set frolicking on the Cote d'Azur.

PHOTO: MARTY SOHL.

founded new companies include Arthur Mitchell (Dance Theatre of Harlem), Edward Villella (Miami City Ballet), and husband-and-wife team, Kent Stowell and Francia Russell (Pacific Northwest Ballet). Other companies, such as the Boston Ballet, Houston Ballet, and Atlanta Ballet, regularly perform Balanchine choreography.

The costs of maintaining such companies are overwhelming to all but the most stouthearted and determined directors. Robert Joffrey was an outstanding example of success at great odds. Beginning in 1954 with six dancers, the Robert Joffrey Ballet toured in a station wagon, presenting a repertory of four Joffrey works, performed in borrowed costumes to taped music. By the 1960s, the company had twenty dancers, a ten-piece orchestra, and funding from private foundations. Continuing to expand during the next twenty years, it came to share popularity ranking with NYCB and ABT. Joffrey, who died in 1988, expected his dancers to perform as individuals in ballets of many diverse styles and periods, whether composed by his prolific assistant director, Gerald Arpino, now in charge of the company, or by visiting artists from the modern dance tradition, such as Twyla Tharp and Laura Dean. Revivals from the Diaghilev era and from Kurt Jooss's expressionistic European ballets of the 1930s have added to the eclectic nature of the repertory. High performance standards are maintained through the company school (American Dance Center in New York City) and by an apprentice company, the Joffrey II Dancers. A pioneering effort was the establishment of a joint base of operations—New York and Los Angeles—whereby the Joffrey Ballet became the first two-city company and the Cleveland–San Jose Ballet later became another. A notable survivor of financial crises is Feld Ballets/NY, a smaller showcase company for the versatile, stylistic choreographic talents of its founder-director, Eliot Feld. But many a creative entrepreneur has had to be satisfied with establishing a small concert group whose members support themselves by means other than performing—all clearly professionals in every sense except that they do not receive a salary commensurate with the minimum required by the American Guild of Musical Artists (AGMA), the union for dancers in ballet, modern companies, or opera. Other choreographers and

The Joffrey Ballet repertory includes several works created for the company by modern dance choreographers. In 1982 Laura Dean composed both the movement and music for *Fire*, here performed by Patricia Brown and Luis Perez.

PHOTO: HERBERT MIGDOLL.

dancers, finding the Broadway stage, films, and television more reliable for earning a decent wage, have helped to make the musical comedy perhaps America's greatest contribution to the theater and to create new audiences by introducing dance to the television screen.

Most companies — large or small, professional or semiprofessional — made a go of it or not according to the Diaghilev method: Tour a lot and try to make up deficits by soliciting gifts from wealthy patrons. Even this usually failed to bring in enough money, and most director-choreographers saved themselves and their companies by teaching.

Gradually, large foundations have been attracted to dance. In 1963 large grants were given by the Ford Foundation, principally to the NYCB and its School of American Ballet, but with some support channeled to certain Balanchine-approved regional companies. Finally, aid began to come from government through the National Endowment for the Arts and from state arts councils, although always vulnerable to economic trends and priorities set by new administrations.

Fine professional (high standards/serious students) ballet schools are found in almost all large cities, and practically every phone book in the country lists at least one ballet studio in its yellow pages. During the 1960s and 1970s, college and university dance major programs, initially modern-dance oriented and supported in physical education departments, eagerly added ballet courses to their curricula and began a gradual relocation into fine arts departments. Professional dancers are being attracted to university faculties, where it is becoming less and less the case of one college-trained teacher turning out another college-trained teacher. The professional dance world and the academic dance world are profiting from the exchange, as ballet and modern dance are benefiting from mutual attractions and understandings. No longer can a modern dancer ignore ballet technique, nor can a ballet dancer remain "untainted" by other dance forms.

The United States enjoys a prominence in the current jet age of dance. A good New York review is as prized as a Paris review once was. Companies from far shores come for a New York season and often a tour of other cities. Moscow's Bolshoi Ballet was perhaps the most eagerly awaited visitor, making an enormously successful New York debut in 1959. Its prima ballerina, Galina Ulanova, had trained with Agrippina Vaganova in her method that now is the basis for ballet education in many countries. Vaganova's 1934 textbook *Basic Principles of Classical Ballet*[37] shows her amalgam of the French and Italian traditions that became the basis of much Russian teaching. In 1959, American audiences were stunned by Bolshoi virtuosity, especially the elevation and strength of its male dancers, who could carry their partners overhead in effortless lifts supported by only one hand. Since then, dance exchanges between the two countries have had interesting by-products, including the greater appreciation of male dancing in the West and a slimmer ballet silhouette for dancers in the East.

An example of today's international dance scene is the career of Nicolaj Hübbe, who trained at the ballet school of the Royal Danish Ballet and at age twenty was appointed principal dancer with the company. He is shown here in the role of James in *La Sylphide*, a version of Filippo Taglioni's ballet created by August Bournonville that has remained in the repertory of the Royal Danish Ballet since 1836. In 1992 Hübbe left Copenhagen to join the New York City Ballet, where he will be featured in quite a different repertory, one largely dominated by the neoclassic ballets of George Balanchine.

PHOTO: DAVID AMZALLAG.

It is the age of the guest artist, who can jet from capital to capital for one-night appearances and a hefty check. Good choreographers are always in demand, crisscrossing the globe from one assignment to another. Fortunately, more permanent residencies sometimes ensue, such as at the Nederlands Dans Theater, where director Jiří Kylián, a Czechoslovakian, has developed his lyrical, wind-swept choreographic style. Another example is William Forsythe, an American whose innovative, startling choreography has matured during his directorship of the Frankfurt Ballet in Germany.

171

The New York Baroque Dance Company is frequently invited to perform in revivals of eighteenth-century operas, such as this production of *Orfeo ed Euridice* by the German composer Christoph Gluck (1761). Although ballet was an integral part of eighteenth-century operas, few opera choreographies survive in notation. Artistic director and dancer, Catherine Turocy, bases her choreography and staging on careful research of eighteenth-century dance, music, costumes, and stage practices.
PHOTO: LOIS GREENFIELD.

Even as today's choreographers explore the possibilities of ballet's technical range and theatrical venue, other contemporary dancer-choreographers seek to reconstruct ballet's historical past. For example, several companies specialize in dances from the baroque era, which they have restored from the notation system (*chorégraphie*) of the time. The New York Baroque Dance Company, directed by Catherine Turocy, and Ris et Danceries, directed by Francine Lancelot in Paris, are two such historical dance ensembles. Using a variety of reconstruction techniques, Pierre Lacotte recently has mounted a number of ballets from the romantic era, in one case bringing back to the stage of the Paris Opéra much of the long-lost choreography of Filippo Taglioni's *La Sylphide*.

Although ballet developed from the culture of the Western world (as such, it meets the criteria for an ethnic dance form, according to anthropologist Joanne

Kealiinohomoku),[38] it is now also a part of the rich dance offerings of Japan, China, Hong Kong, and many other Asian-Pacific cultures. Ballet has become a truly international art form, with annual competitions for aspiring artists (much like those for young pianists) held in ballet centers from Moscow to Jackson, Mississippi.

It seems that ballet has come a very long way from its early days as royal entertainment in the court of Louis XIV. But was it really so long ago? To trace one dancer's heritage, you can look, for example, at the ballet "genealogy" of the

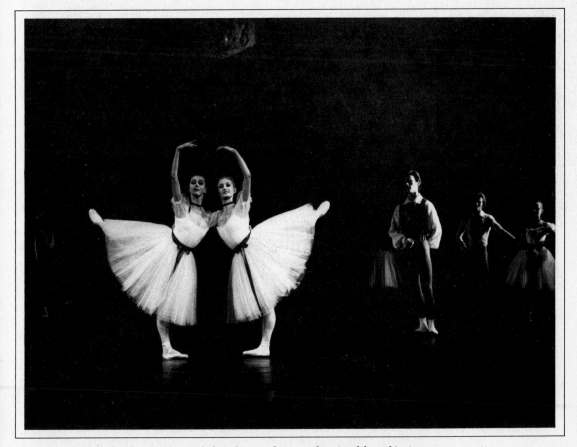

The tradition of the ballet classroom, passed along from teacher to student, is celebrated in August Bournonville's homage to one of his teachers, Auguste Vestris. This scene is from Act I of Bournonville's *The Conservatoire or A Marriage Advertisement* (1849), performed by Royal Danish Ballet dancers Rose Gad and Christina Olsson, as the students, and Lloyd Riggins as their approving ballet master.

PHOTO: DAVID AMZALLAG.

author of the book you are now reading. Foremost among her (my) teachers were Margaret Craske and Dolores Mitrovich, each of whom studied with Enrico Cecchetti (Craske in England and Mitrovich in Italy). Cecchetti studied with Giovanni Lepri, a disciple of Blasis, who in turn had worked with Dauberval, a dancer with Noverre. Noverre trained with Dupré, who had worked with Pécour, the ballet master who succeeded Beauchamps at the Paris Opéra. Beauchamps gave dance lessons to Louis XIV.

That is a span of only ten ballet generations. The ballet family tree has many branches, but it is not so very tall after all, and every ballet dancer today can connect somewhere to one of those branches. Even though ballet roots go very deep (some like to say back to ritual dances of ancient cultures), its fascinating/ exasperating, logical/unnatural, tender/provocative, balanced/venturesome dance technique has a relatively brief history.

And it is a highly personal history. One pair of feet has demonstrated for another pair, one hand has guided another body, one voice has encouraged another soul, one set of muscles has remembered what a mind may have forgotten. Ballet has not been, cannot be, transmitted alone from book or machine. It is an experience that must be lived. Ten generations have so lived it, studied it, performed it, taught it, redirected it. We can look forward to more.

**NOTES**

1. The undated Domenico manuscript is in the Bibliothèque Nationale, Paris. *Saltare* was a term implying pantomime or representative dance by professional performers; the term came to mean jumping or leaping. *Chorea* was a term later identified with *carole*, line or closed-circle dances with participants holding hands; these dances could be stately and stepped or lively with hops. These and other early dance terms are discussed by Ingrid Brainard in "Dance of the Middle Ages and Early Renaissance," in *The New Grove Dictionary of Music and Musicians*, vol. 5 (London: Macmillan, 1980), 180–85.

2. Ingrid Brainard, "Domenico da Piacenza," in *The New Grove Dictionary of Music and Musicians*, vol. 5 (London: Macmillan, 1980), 332–33.

3. Plato, *The Laws*, VII, 814, in *The Dialogues of Plato*, trans. B. Jowett (Oxford, 1953), 383.

4. First established at the University of Wisconsin in Madison by Margaret H'Doubler in 1921.

5. Quintilian, *Institutio oratorio*, 11.3.88, trans. Frank W. D. Ries in "Roman Pantomime: Practice and Politics," *Dance Scope* 12 (Fall/Winter 1977–78): 40.

6. Clement of Alexandria, referring to a hymn in the Apocryphal Acts of St. John. Quoted in Kathy Meyer-Baer, *Music of the Spheres and the Dance of Death* (Princeton: N.J.: Princeton University Press, 1970), 35–36.

7. Régine Kunzle, "In Search of L'Académie Royale de Danse," *York Dance Review* 7 (Spring 1978): 7.

8. *Ibid.*, 8.

9. *Ibid.*

10. Quoted in "Fifteenth- and Early Sixteenth-Century Court Dances," in *Institute of Court Dances of the Renaissance and Baroque Periods*, ed. Juana de Laban (New York: Dance Notation Bureau, 1972), 4.

11. *Pavana*, an adjective meaning "of Padua," implies that the dance took its name from that town. Some scholars believe the dance term (also *pavan, pavane*) derives from *pavón* (Spanish for

peacock), indicating a relationship between the dignified, yet colorful dance and the elegant spread of a peacock's tail. *Gagliarda* (also *galliard, gaillarde*) means "vigorous, robust." *Saltarello*, or "little hop," is a dance form sometimes called *pas de brabant* or *alta danza*. *Canario* (also canary, *canarie*) is thought to be a dance form from the Canary Islands introduced to Spain in the sixteenth century and thence to the rest of the Continent.

12. Thoinot Arbeau, *Orchesography* (Langres, 1589), trans. Mary Stewart Evans, ed. Julia Sutton (New York: Dover, 1967), 81.

13. Quoted in *Le Balet Comique de la Royne*, 1581, trans. Carol and Lander MacClintock (American Institute of Musicology, 1971), 33.

14. A Greek mathematician and physicist, living 287?–212 B.C.

15. *Le Balet Comique, op. cit.*, 90–91.

16. James Miller, "The Philosophical Background of Renaissance Dance," *York Dance Review* 51 (Spring 1976): 3.

17. Quoted in Régine Kunzle, "Pierre Beauchamps: The Illustrious Unknown Choreographer: Part II," *Dance Scope* (Fall/Winter 1974–75), 36.

18. Pierre Rameau, *The Dancing Master* (Paris, 1725), trans. Cyril W. Beaumont (New York: Dance Horizons, 1970), 5.

19. Joan Wildeblood, *The Polite World* (London: Davis-Poynter, 1973), 94.

20. Rameau (see Note 18) provides the most accessible information.

21. Exact translations and/or derivations of names of dances are often impossible to make and sometimes shed little light on the dance form itself. For instance, the late seventeenth–early eighteenth-century *courante* was majestic and grave, unlike the livelier *coranto* or *corrente* forms of the preceding era. The terms, however, can be translated as "running or flowing." Some scholars suggest the name *minuet* or *menuet* may have derived from the French "*menu*" (slender, small), perhaps referring to the small steps of the dance.

22. Quoted in Selma Jeanne Cohen, ed., *Dance as a Theatre Art* (New York: Harper & Row, 1974), 51.

23. Quoted in Lincoln Kirstein, *Dance: A Short History of Classic Theatrical Dancing* (New York: Dance Horizons, 1969), 209.

24. Jean Georges Noverre, *Letters on Dancing and Ballets*, trans. Cyril W. Beaumont (New York: Dance Horizons, 1968), 29, 99.

25. *Ibid.*, 117.

26. *Ibid.*, 99.

27. Quoted in Kirstein (see Note 22), 236.

28. Jack Anderson, *Ballet & Modern Dance, A Concise History* (Princeton, N.J.: Princeton Book, 1986), 65.

29. Translation by Mary Stewart Evans (New York: Dover, 1968).

30. *Ibid.*, 46.

31. *Théorie de la gymnastique de la danse théatrale* (Paris, 1859). Translated excerpts in Cohen (see Note 22), 71–77.

32. Republished in *Studies in Dance History*, a publication of the Society of Dance History Scholars, as Volume II, No. 1, Fall/Winter 1990.

33. Auguste Bournonville, *My Theatre Life* (Copenhagen, 1848–1878), trans. Patricia N. McAndrew (Middletown, Ct.: Wesleyan University Press, 1979), 581–82.

34. (New York: Dance Horizons, 1977).

35. Cyril W. Beaumont and Stanislas Idzikowski, *A Manual of the Theory and Practice of Classical Theatrical Dancing* (New York: Dover, 1975).

36. Arlene Croce, "Mikhail Baryshnikov," in *The Dance Anthology*, ed. Cobbett Steinberg (New York: New American Library, 1980), 121–22.

37. First published in Leningrad, Vaganova's book has been translated by Anatole Chujoy and republished by Dover (New York, 1969).

38. Joanne Kealiinohomoku, "An Anthropologist Looks at Ballet as a Form of Ethnic Dance," *Impulse* (1969–70): 24–33.

# SELECTED READING

**GENERAL REFERENCE**

Balanchine, George, and Francis Mason. *101 Stories of the Great Ballets*. Garden City, N.Y.: Doubleday, Dolphin Books, 1975.

Brinson, Peter, and Clement Crisp. *Ballet and Dance: A Guide to the Repertory*. London: David & Charles, 1980.

Clark, Mary, and David Vaughan, eds. *The Encyclopedia of Dance and Ballet*. New York: Putnam, 1977.

Cohen-Stratyner, and Barbara Naomi. *Biographical Dictionary of Dance*. New York: Schirmer Books, 1982.

Grant, Gail. *Technical Manual and Dictionary of Classical Ballet*. New York: Dover, 1982.

Koegler, Horst. *The Concise Oxford Dictionary of Ballet*. London: Oxford University Press, 1982.

Steinberg, Cobbett, ed. *The Dance Anthology*. New York: New American Library, 1980.


**TECHNIQUE**

Bazarova, Nadezjhda, and Varvara Mey, eds. *Alphabet of Classical Dance*. London: Dance Books, 1983.

Beaumont, Cyril, and Stanislas Idzikowski. *A Manual of the Theory and Practice of Classical Theatrical Dancing* (rev. ed.). New York: Dover, 1975.

Bruhn, Erik, and Lillian Moore. *Bournonville and Ballet Technique*. London: Adam & Charles Black, 1961.

Glasstone, Richard. *Better Ballet*. Cranbury, N.J.: Barnes, 1977.

Hammond, Sandra Noll. *Ballet: Beyond the Basics*. Palo Alto: Mayfield, 1982.

Karsavina, Tamara. *Classical Ballet: The Flow of Movement*. London: Adam & Charles Black, 1962.

LaPointe-Crump, Janice D. *In Balance: The Fundamentals of Ballet*. Dubuque, Iowa: Brown, 1985.

Paskevska, Anna. *Ballet: From the First Plié to Mastery, An Eight-Year Course*. Princeton, N.J.: Princeton Book, 1990.

Prudhomme, Germaine. *The Book of Ballet*, trans. Katherine Corsan. Englewood Cliffs, N.J.: Prentice-Hall, 1976.

Stuart, Muriel, and Lincoln Kirstein. *The Classic Ballet*. New York: Knopf, 1982.

Vaganova, Agrippina. *Basic Principles of Classical Ballet*. New York: Dover, 1969.

## CARE OF THE BODY

Alexander, F. M. *The Universal Constant in Living*. New York: Dutton, 1941.

Arnheim, Daniel D. *Dance Injuries: Their Prevention and Cure* (3rd ed.). Princeton, N.J.: Princeton Book, 1991.

Bartenieff, Irmgard, with Doris Lewis. *Body Movement: Coping with the Environment*. New York: Gordon & Breach, 1980.

Berardi, Gigi. *Finding Balance: Fitness & Training for a Lifetime in Dance*. Princeton, N.J.: Princeton Book, 1990.

Chmelar, Robin D., and Sally S. Fitt. *Diet: A Complete Guide to Nutrition & Weight Control*. Princeton, N.J.: Princeton Book, 1990.

Featherstone, Donald F. *Dancing Without Danger*. South Brunswick and New York: Barnes, 1970.

Feldenkrais, Moshe. *Awareness Through Movement*. New York: Harper & Row, 1972.

Fitt, Sally S. *Dance Kinesiology*. New York: Schirmer Books, 1988.

Ryan, Allan J., M.D., and Robert E. Stephens, Ph.D., eds. *The Healthy Dancer: Dance Medicine for Dancers. Selected Articles from Dance Medicine. A Comprehensive Guide*. Princeton, N.J.: Princeton Book, 1990.

Sparger, Celia. *Anatomy and Ballet*. London: Adam & Charles Black, 1982.

Spilken, Terry L., M.D. *The Dancer's Foot Book*. Princeton, N.J.: Princeton Book, 1990.

Sweigard, Lulu. *Human Movement Potential, Its Ideokinetic Facilitation*. New York: Dodd, Mead, 1974.

Vincent, L. M. *Competing with the Sylph: Dancers and the Pursuit of the Ideal Body Form*. New York: Andrews & McMeel, 1980.

———. *The Dancer's Book of Health*. Kansas City, Kans.: Andrews & McMeel, 1978.

d'Amboise, Christopher. *A Year in the Life of a Dancer*. Garden City, N.Y.: Doubleday, 1982.

Glasstone, Richard. *Male Dancing as a Career*. London: Kaye & Ward, 1980.

Gordon, Suzanne. *Off Balance: The Real World of Ballet*. New York: Pantheon Books, 1983.

Jacob, Ellen. *Dancing: A Guide for the Dancer You Can Be*. Reading, Mass.: Addison-Wesley, 1981.

Martins, Peter. *Far from Denmark*. Boston: Little, Brown, 1982.

Mazo, Joseph. *Dance Is a Contact Sport*. New York: Da Capo Press, 1974.

Villella, Edward, with Larry Kaplan. *Prodigal Son. Dancing for Balanchine in a World of Pain and Magic*. New York: Simon & Schuster, 1992.

Whitehill, Angela, and William Noble. *The Young Professional's Book of Ballet: From Student to Ballerina*. Princeton, N.J.: Princeton Book, 1990.

## BALLET VIEWING

Cohen, Selma Jeanne. *Next Week Swan Lake: Reflections on Dance and Dancers*. Middletown, Conn.: Wesleyan University Press, 1982.

Croce, Arlene, *Going to the Dance*. New York: Knopf, 1982.

——. *Afterimages*. New York: Random House, Vintage Books, 1979.

——. *Sight Lines*. New York: Knopf, 1987.

Denby, Edwin. *Dance Writings*. New York: Knopf, 1986.

McDonagh, Don. *How to Enjoy the Ballet*. Garden City, N.Y.: Doubleday, Dolphin Books, 1980.

Siegel, Marcia B. *At the Vanishing Point*. New York: Saturday Review Press, 1973.

——. *Watching the Dance Go By*. Boston: Houghton Mifflin, 1977.

## HISTORY

Anderson, Jack. *Ballet & Modern Dance: A Concise History* (2nd ed.). Princeton, N.J.: Princeton Book, 1992.

Au, Susan. *Ballet and Modern Dance*. New York: Thames & Hudson, 1988.

Chazin-Bennahum, Judith. *Dance in the Shadow of the Guillotine*. Carbondale: Southern Illinois University Press, 1988.

Cohen, Selma Jeanne. *Dance as a Theatre Art: Selected Readings in Dance History*. New York: Harper & Row, 1974.

Garafola, Lynn. *Diaghilev's Ballets Russes*. New York: Oxford University Press, 1989.

Hilton, Wendy. *Dance of Court & Theater: The French Noble Style, 1690–1725*. Princeton, N.J.: Princeton Book, 1981.

Jowitt, Deborah. *Time and the Dancing Image*. New York: Morrow, 1988.

Kirstein, Lincoln. *Dance: A Short History of Classic Theatrical Dancing*. New York: Dance Horizons, 1977.

Kraus, Richard, Sarah Alberti Chapman, and Brenda Dixon. *History of the Dance in Art and Education* (3rd ed.). Englewood Cliffs, N.J.: Prentice-Hall, 1991.

Moore, Lillian. *Echoes of American Ballet*. Brooklyn: Dance Horizons, 1976.

Swift, Mary Grace. *The Art of Dance in the U.S.S.R.*. Notre Dame, Ind.: University of Notre Dame, 1968.

Winter, Marian Hannah. *The Pre-Romantic Ballet*. New York: Pitman, 1974.

## MOSTLY PICTORIAL

Clarke, Mary, and Clement Crisp. *Ballet Art from the Renaissance to the Present*. New York: Potter, 1978.

France, Charles Engell. *Baryshnikov at Work*. New York: Knopf, 1979.

Jurgensen, Knud A. *The Bournonville Ballets: A Photographic Record 1844–1933*. Princeton, N.J.: Princeton Book, 1987.

Kahn, Albert E. *Days with Ulanova*. New York: Simon & Schuster, 1962.

Kirstein, Lincoln. *Four Centuries of Ballet: Fifty Masterworks*. New York: Dover, 1984.

Kochno, Boris. *Diaghilev and the Ballets Russes*. New York: Harper & Row 1979.

Migel, Parmenia. *Great Ballet Prints of the Romantic Era*. New York: Dover, 1981.

Moore, Lillian. *Images of the Dance*. New York: N.Y. Public Library, 1965.

## PERIODICALS

*Ballet Review* (quarterly), 150 Claremont Ave., New York, N.Y. 10027.

*Dance Chronicle* (three times yearly), Marcel Dekker Journals, P.O. Box 10018, Church Street Station, New York, N.Y. 10249.

*Dance Magazine* (monthly), 33 W. 60th St., New York, N.Y. 10023.

*Dance Research* (biannual), Oxford University Press, Pinkhill House, Southfield Road, Eynsham, Oxford OX8 1JJ, U.K.

*Studies in Dance History* (biannual), Society of Dance History Scholars, Princeton Periodicals, P.O. Box 380, Pennington, N.J. 08534.

## VIDEOS

The following videos, primarily of ballet training, are available from Princeton Book Co., P.O. Box 57, Pennington, N.J. 08534.

*Ballet Class for Beginners*. David Howard, instructor.

*Ballet Class: Intermediate-Advanced*. David Howard, instructor.

*The Ballet Workout*. Melissa Lowe, instructor.

*The Children of Theatre Street* (Kirov Ballet School). Princess Grace of Monaco, narrator.

*The Video Dictionary of Classical Ballet*. Merrill Ashley (NYCB), Denise Jackson (Joffrey), Kevin McKenzie (ABT), and Georgina Parkinson (ABT), dancers. The following video introduces a supplementary training program for ballet dancers as well as others "who want to keep fit and in touch with their bodies."

*Rommett Floor-Barre Technique: A Method to Develop and Refine Ballet Technique*. New York: Zena Rommett, 1991.

# TECHNICAL TERMS INDEX

Page numbers refer to major explanations of technical terms. Boldfaced numbers refer to illustrations. Additional entries for these terms are given in the General Index.

183

# GENERAL INDEX

Boldfaced numbers refer to illustrations.